CAMBRIDGE
UNIVERSITY PRESS

Cambridge IGCSE™
English as a
Second Language

EXAM PREPARATION AND PRACTICE

Katia Carter & Tim Carter

Shaftesbury Road, Cambridge CB2 8EA, United Kingdom

One Liberty Plaza, 20th Floor, New York, NY 10006, USA

477 Williamstown Road, Port Melbourne, VIC 3207, Australia

314–321, 3rd Floor, Plot 3, Splendor Forum, Jasola District Centre, New Delhi – 110025, India

103 Penang Road, #05–06/07, Visioncrest Commercial, Singapore 238467

Cambridge University Press & Assessment is part of the University of Cambridge.

It furthers the University's mission by disseminating knowledge in the pursuit of education, learning and research at the highest international levels of excellence.

www.cambridge.org
Information on this title: www.cambridge.org/9781009300247

First published 2017
Second edition 2023

20 19 18 17 16 15 14 13 12 11 10 9 8 7 6 5 4

Printed in Malaysia by Vivar Printing

A catalogue record for this publication is available from the British Library

ISBN 978-1-009-30024-7 Paperback + Cambridge GO edition (2 years)

Cambridge University Press & Assessment has no responsibility for the persistence or accuracy of URLs for external or third-party internet websites referred to in this publication, and does not guarantee that any content on such websites is, or will remain, accurate or appropriate.

All exam-style questions and sample answers have been written by the authors.

This resource has not been through the Cambridge International endorsement process. The practice tests and mark schemes included in this resource have been written by the authors and provide students with an opportunity for additional practice. Questions in this resource will not appear in examinations. In examinations the way marks are awarded may be different. Any references to assessment and/or assessment preparation are the publisher's interpretation of the syllabus requirements. While the publishers have made every attempt to ensure that advice on the qualification and its assessment is accurate, the official syllabus, specimen assessment materials and any associated assessment guidance materials produced by the awarding body are the only authoritative source of information and should always be referred to for definitive guidance.

> Contents

The digital resource contains:

Answer key

Audioscripts

Example multiple-choice answer sheet for Listening paper

> Introduction

Dear student,

Thank you for choosing the Cambridge IGCSE™ English as a Second Language Exam Preparation and Practice book to help you prepare for your exams.

The whole book follows the 'test – teach – test' approach. This means that first you test yourself to see what you already know. The next stage is 'teaching'. This means we will help you identify the areas you need to improve. You will also look at your own mistakes and learn useful techniques and language structures to help you work on your weaker areas. And finally, you will do the same type of exam task, or an exam question, to test yourself again to see if your skills have improved.

The book is divided into **three sections** focusing on the following skills:

- Section 1: Reading and writing

- Section 2: Listening

- Section 3: Speaking.

Each section is then divided into **four units**. Each unit has a different focus to help you with different aspects of each exam:

- **About the exam**: Units 1.1, 2.1 and 3.1

These units focus on the format of the exam. You will find out how many parts there are in each paper and what you are required to do in each one.

- **Exam techniques**: Units 1.2, 2.2 and 3.2 (Tests 1 and 2)

These units focus on how to best approach each exam task and what you should do before, while and after doing it. There are useful tips to help you improve your performance in these exam tasks. You will see what the examiners are looking for in your answers and will look at other students' sample answers. We will show you common mistakes that other students make so that you can avoid making the same mistakes yourself. At the end of each exam task, there are suggestions about what else you can do to improve your skills even further.

- **Language focus**: Units 1.3, 2.3 and 3.3 (Test 3)

These units focus on important vocabulary and grammar that is needed when answering exam questions.

- **Test yourself**: Units 1.4, 2.4 and 3.4 (Test 4)

These units test whether your performance has improved as a result of what you have learnt in the previous units. You will be asked to do a complete test under exam conditions to see whether you are ready for the real exam.

Throughout the book you will be encouraged to reflect on your own performance in individual exam tasks. This is to ensure that you can identify your strengths and weaknesses, which will help you plan what you still need to practise before the exam.

To track your progress for individual exam tasks and questions, we have included a progress chart at the start of the book. Please use this chart to fill in your scores from individual exercises you have done to see how well you are progressing. When you have finished doing all the sections and exercises in this book, you can look at this chart and easily identify which skills and exercises you still need to practise and whether you are fully ready for the Cambridge IGCSE English as a Second Language exams.

Our main aim when writing this book was to make the Cambridge IGCSE English as a Second Language assessment as clear as possible for you and to show you what is expected of you. We also want to give you the right learning 'tools' so that you can become a more confident and independent student because independent students can take on any learning challenge and be successful in whatever exam they choose to take in the future.

We hope you will find this book useful, but will also enjoy using it.

Good luck on your learning journey.

Katia and Tim Carter
The authors

> How to use this book

TIP

You will find these tips throughout the book. They provide useful techniques and advice to help you improve your performance in exams.

Reflection

You will find these features after each Test 1 exam task in Units 1.2, 2.2 and 3.2. They tell you how to answer each exam-style question most successfully.

Learn from mistakes

These sections show common mistakes real students make in listening, reading, writing and speaking exams. These sections also contain real students' sample answers.

LANGUAGE FOCUS

This feature appears either as a box, or a whole section after the Test 3 exam tasks in Units 1.3, 2.3 and 3.3. They will help you identify the key grammar and vocabulary needed to answer exam questions successfully.

Model answer

You will find model answers for the writing part of the exam in Unit 1.3 and in the answer key for Units 1.2, 1.3 and 1.4. These are examples of good answers to provide you with models for your own writing.

CHECK YOUR PROGRESS

These features appear throughout the book. They will remind you to reflect on your progress so far. They will also encourage you to think about how much you have learnt and whether there is anything that you still need to improve.

Develop your skills

This feature appears at the end of each Test 2 exam task in Units 1.2, 2.2 and 3.2. These boxes contain a list of activities and suggestions to help you further develop the skills that you are tested on in the assessment.

Available in the digital resource

Where you see this icon, an **audio track** is available in the digital resource. The number shown in the icon is the audio track number. (You will need to play each audio track twice in Unit 2.3.)

Where you see this icon, a **video** is available in the digital resource. The number shown in the icon is the video number.

At the end of the listening exam, you will be asked to transfer your answers onto a separate multiple-choice answer sheet. You can download an **example multiple-choice answer sheet** from the digital resource.

Audioscripts for all audio tracks in this book can be downloaded from the digital resource.

You will find three different multiple-choice quizzes in the digital resource. The quizzes cover grammar, vocabulary and pronunciation.

> Progress chart: tracking sheet

Use the progress chart to record your scores for individual exam-style exercises in each test, 1–4. This chart will help you see if your performance in individual exam-style exercises is improving. When you have completed all four tests, decide what you need to do next and fill in the last column with one of these conclusions:

Yes   (I am now ready to take the exam)

Almost   (I still need a bit more practice)

Not quite   (I still need a lot of practice)

The progress chart will also help you to plan your revision timetable because you will be able to see which parts of the exam you need to give priority to before you take the assessment.

Reading and Writing paper	Total number of marks	Your score in **Test 1**	Your score in **Test 2**	Your score in **Test 3**	Your score in **Test 4**	Are you now ready for the exam?
Exercise 1 (Questions 1–6)	8 marks					
Exercise 2 (Question 7)	9 marks					
Exercise 3 (Questions 8–9)	7 marks					
Exercise 4 (Questions 10–15)	6 marks					
Exercise 5 (Question 16)	15 marks					
Exercise 6 (Question 17)	15 marks					

Listening paper	Total number of marks	Your score in Test 1	Your score in Test 2	Your score in Test 3	Your score in Test 4	Are you now ready for the exam?
Exercise 1 (Questions 1–8)	8 marks					
Exercise 2 (Question 9–18)	10 marks					
Exercise 3 (Questions 19–26)	8 marks					
Exercise 4 (Questions 27–32)	6 marks					
Exercise 5 (Questions 33–40)	8 marks					
Speaking paper	Total number of marks	Your score in Test 1	Your score in Test 2	Your score in Test 3	Your score in Test 4	Are you now ready for the exam?
Part 1: Interview Part 2: Short talk Part 3: Discussion	40 marks					

To help you decide if you are ready for the real exams, here is a little help. Look at the descriptions in the following table. Which one is the closest to what you can do in each skill? When you find a match in the description column, put a tick next to it. Where are most of your ticks? Do you think you are now ready for the exams?

Are you now ready for the **Reading** exam?

	Descriptions
Yes	• You can provide correct answers to almost all questions in all the reading exercises. • You can complete all the reading exercises within the time limit.
Almost	• You can provide correct answers to most questions in all the reading exercises. • You find it difficult to complete some of the reading exercises within the time limit.
Not quite	• You can only provide correct answers to half of the questions in all the reading exercises. • You take a long time to read the texts and you often do not complete the reading exercises.

Are you now ready for the **Writing** exam?

	Descriptions
Yes	• You can complete the task fully, within the time limit. • You know what register and style is appropriate for different types of writing. • Your answers are well developed, well organised into paragraphs and you link the ideas with a good range of linking words. • You often use complex structures and a very good range of vocabulary. • You only make very few minor errors.
Almost	• You can complete the task within the time limit but occasionally you forget to include some details from the exam question. • Sometimes you are not sure what register and style you should use for different types of writing. • You develop some of your ideas, organise them into paragraphs and link the ideas using a range of linking words. • You use mostly simple structures and common vocabulary. • You make quite a few errors, but your writing can still be understood.
Not quite	• You find it hard to complete the task within the time limit *and/or* your answer has some missing details. • You are not sure what register or style to use for different types of writing. • Your answers are very short with almost no development, you rarely use paragraphs and you only use very simple linking words. • You only use short simple sentences and very common vocabulary. • You make quite a few errors and this sometimes makes your writing difficult to understand.

Are you now ready for the **Listening** exam?

	Descriptions
Yes	• You can provide correct answers to almost all questions in all the listening exercises. • You understand almost everything in the listening practice exams.
Almost	• You can provide correct answers to most questions in all the listening exercises. • You occasionally find it difficult to understand some of the information in the listening practice exams.
Not quite	• You can provide correct answers to most questions in Exercises 1 and 3, where you listen for specific detail. You can provide correct answers to around half of the questions in Exercises 2, 4 and 5, where you listen for implied information as well as specific detail. • You often find it difficult to understand some of the information in the listening practice exams. • You sometimes get lost and you do not know which question you are on in longer talks or interviews.

Are you now ready for the **Speaking** exam?

	Descriptions
Yes	• You can take part in conversations and discussions about more challenging topics independently with no, or very little, help. • You give answers that are well developed and relevant. • You can use a range of language structures, including more complex grammar and precise vocabulary. • You only make very few minor errors. • You sound clear and also use intonation patterns in your speech to make what you mean clearer.
Almost	• You can take part in everyday conversations and discussions, but you still find challenging topics difficult and sometimes need help. • Some of your answers are developed, especially the ones about everyday topics. • You try to use some complex grammar and a range of vocabulary, but sometimes you make errors when using these. • Occasionally, you mispronounce words, but people can mostly understand what you are saying. You do not usually use intonation patterns in your speech.
Not quite	• You can only take part in simple everyday conversations and you still need support with these. • Your answers are very short and sometimes not relevant because you do not always understand what you are asked about. • You try to use simple grammar in your sentences, but these are sometimes incomplete. • You can only use simple vocabulary, but you sometimes have to stop to think about the words you want to use. • You make quite a few errors and do not always sound clear. This makes it difficult for others to understand what you are saying.

> Assessment criteria for writing and speaking

The following criteria are designed to help you understand how your work will be graded. (We have simplified the assessment criteria used by Cambridge Assessment International Education in the Cambridge IGCSE English as a Second Language exams.)

Writing: Exercises 5 and 6

Give a separate content mark and language mark by deciding which band is the best fit for each. (The content and language marks can be different if necessary.) If all of the criteria of the band are met, give the upper mark; if it meets some of the criteria, give the lower mark.

Give 1 or 2 marks for content to very short answers. Give 0 marks for content and language to completely irrelevant answers.

Content	
Description	Marks
The answer: • addresses the task completely • only includes content that is relevant to the task • uses an appropriate format and register throughout • shows an excellent understanding of purpose and audience • is very well developed • meets the word count requirement.	5–6
The answer: • mainly addresses the task • mainly includes content that is relevant to the task • uses mainly appropriate format and register • shows a good understanding of purpose and audience • is mainly well developed • meets the word count requirement.	3–4
The answer: • partially addresses the task • includes some content that is not relevant to the task • produces text with an inconsistent or inappropriate format and register • shows a lack of understanding of purpose and audience • shows minimal development • is below the required word count.	1–2
No creditable content	0

Language	
Description	**Marks**
The answer: • uses a broad range of both common and uncommon vocabulary • uses a broad range of simple and complex structures • uses language that is almost always accurate; any errors are in less common vocabulary or complex structures, and do not affect the reader's comprehension • is organised effectively • uses a broad range of linking words and devices.	7–9
The answer: • uses a range of common vocabulary, with some examples of less common vocabulary • uses a broad range of simple structures, and tries to use some complex structures • uses language that is mainly accurate; errors are mostly in less common vocabulary or complex structures, and do not affect the reader's comprehension • is reasonably well organised • uses a range of linking words and devices.	4–6
The answer: • uses only common vocabulary • uses only simple structures • uses language that is sometimes difficult to understand, due to errors in common vocabulary and simple structures • shows only a basic attempt at organisation • uses a small range of linking words and devices.	1–3
No creditable content	0

Speaking

When using the marking criteria, consider the student's responses to all assessed Parts 1–3. Select a mark from 0–10 for each of grammar, vocabulary, development and pronunciation, and then combine them to give a total mark out of 40.

Marks	Grammar	Vocabulary	Development	Pronunciation
9–10	• Student uses a range of simple and complex structures. • Student makes minimal errors in both simple and complex structures. • The meaning is always clear.	• Student can talk about and express opinions on a range of facts and ideas. • Student uses a wide range of vocabulary. • Student can use some vocabulary with precision.	• Student always responds relevantly and develops their ideas. • Student needs no or very little support to maintain communication.	• Student's pronunciation is always clear. • Student often uses intonation effectively to communicate the intended meaning.

7–8	• Student uses a range of simple structures and attempts to use some complex structures. • Student makes minimal errors in simple structures, but more frequent errors in complex structures. • The meaning is always clear despite the errors.	• Student can talk about and express opinions on a range of facts and ideas. • Student uses a reasonable range of vocabulary. • Student uses vocabulary correctly.	• Student responds relevantly and develops most of their ideas. • Student needs occasional support to maintain communication.	• Student can be understood despite some pronunciation issues. • Student sometimes uses intonation effectively to communicate the intended meaning.
5–6	• Student uses a range of simple structures, but complex structures are rarely used. • Student makes some errors in the structures used. • The meaning may sometimes be unclear because of the errors.	• Student can talk about and express opinions on simple facts and ideas. • Student uses a range of vocabulary. • Student uses most vocabulary correctly.	• Student responds relevantly and develops some of their ideas. • Student needs frequent support to maintain communication.	• Student can mostly be understood, but some effort is needed because of pronunciation issues. • Student rarely uses intonation effectively to communicate the intended meaning.
3–4	• Student uses a very limited range of simple structures. • Student makes frequent errors. • The meaning is often unclear because of the errors.	• Student can only talk about and express opinions on basic facts. • Student uses a limited range of vocabulary.	• Student provides some irrelevant responses and rarely develops their ideas. • Student has difficulty maintaining communication despite frequent support.	• Student can rarely be understood, effort is needed because of pronunciation issues. • Student does not use intonation effectively to communicate the intended meaning.
1–2	• Student only uses isolated words or simple short phrases. • The meaning is unclear throughout.	• Student has difficulty talking about and expressing opinions on even the most basic facts. • Student only uses extremely limited and repetitive vocabulary.	• Student only provides very short isolated responses. • Student cannot maintain communication despite frequent support.	• Student has serious pronunciation issues, which lead to a breakdown in communication. • Student does not use any intonation patterns.
0	No answer given	No answer given	No answer given	No answer given

Disclaimer: Please note that these mark schemes have not been produced by Cambridge Assessment International Education. The descriptors are based on Cambridge International's descriptors but have been written by the authors of this resource. If you wish to see the official grade criteria for Cambridge IGCSE English as a Second Language, please visit the Cambridge Assessment International Education website, www.cambridgeinternational.org

> Acknowledgements

The authors and publishers acknowledge the following sources of copyright material and are grateful for the permissions granted. While every effort has been made, it has not always been possible to identify the sources of all the material used, or to trace all copyright holders. If any omissions are brought to our notice, we will be happy to include the appropriate acknowledgements on reprinting.

Thanks to the following for permission to reproduce images:

Cover bhblue/GI; *Reading Test 1, Ex. 1* Adrian Dennis/GI; *Test 2, Ex. 1* Education Images/GI; *Test 1, Ex. 3* CTK/ Alamy Stock Photo; *Test 2, Ex. 3* Vincent Capman/GI; *Test 3, Ex. 1* Media Drum World/Alamy Stock Photo; *Test 3, Ex. 3* Punnawit Suwuttananun/GI; *Test 4, Ex. 1* H. Armstrong Roberts/GI; *Test 4, Ex. 3* Sebastien Micke/GI; *Test 4, Ex. 4* Specker/GI; *Test 4, Ex. 5* JGI/Tom Grill/GI; *Listening Test 1, Ex. 3* Pikselstock/Shutterstock; *Test 2, Ex. 3* Ac_bnphotos/GI; *Test 3, Ex. 1* oxygen/GI; *Test 3, Ex. 3* Olivier Morin/GI; *Test 4, Part 3* Christian Vierig/GI; *Test 4, Part 5* Michal Vojtech; *Speaking, Unit 3.2* SDI Productions/GI; *Unit 3.3* Karelnoppe/Shutterstock; Robert Daly/GI

Key: GI = Getty Images

Unit 1.1: About the exam

How much do you already know about the format of the Reading and Writing exam and what happens during the exam? Can you answer the following questions?

1 How many parts are there in the Reading and Writing exam? .... [1]

2 How much time do you have to complete the whole Reading and Writing exam?

.... [1]

3 Look at the following table. Can you match each exercise with the correct exam task?

.... [6]

TIP

If you are new to the Reading and Writing exam, first go to Unit 1.4 and look at the complete test to see what each section looks like.

Reading and Writing exam		
Exercise 1	A	Informal email You write an informal email to a friend. As part of the task, there are three bullet points with three ideas that you must include in your email.
Exercise 2	B	Multiple choice You read a text and answer six questions, mainly about the writer's ideas, attitudes and opinions. At least one question will test your ability to understand referencing words (e.g. it, them, this). You choose your answer from three options and tick the correct box.
Exercise 3	C	Question-answer reading comprehension You read a text and answer six questions. Most questions require one detail (e.g. name, number, activity). The last question always requires three details, which appear throughout the text (e.g. problems, advice, goals, reasons). You write your answer on the line provided.
Exercise 4	D	Discursive writing (report/review/article/essay) You write an article, an essay, a review or a report, which are mostly semi-formal to formal. Apart from the task, there are also four prompts connected to the task. These prompts will help you think of some ideas for your own written answer but you should also include your own ideas.
Exercise 5	E	Note-taking You read a text and take notes under given headings. There will usually be two or three headings. Each heading may require three or four ideas (e.g. advantages, reasons), which you will find in the text. You need to include seven ideas/examples in total.
Exercise 6	F	Multiple matching You read four (occasionally five) short paragraphs on the same topic (e.g. about people's hobbies) in which different people express their opinions, feelings or attitudes. You then have to match these paragraphs to nine statements by writing the correct letter A, B, C or D next to each statement.

4   What is the total number of marks you can get? .... [1]

5   Do you have to answer all the exercises on the exam paper? .... [1]

6   Do you lose marks if your answer is wrong? .... [1]

7   Can you use a dictionary during the exam? .... [1]

8   Do you have to transfer your answers onto a separate answer sheet at the end

     of the exam? .... [1]

Now go to the answer key for Section 1, Unit 1.1 and check your answers.

Your score: .... out of 13

Now look at the following table. How much do you know about each exercise in the Reading and Writing exam? Can you tick the correct boxes and complete the correct numbers for each exercise? If you do not know the answers, look at the reading and writing test in Unit 1.4 and then complete the table.

Reading and Writing exam in more detail						
	Ex. 1	Ex. 2	Ex. 3	Ex. 4	Ex. 5	Ex. 6
Which exercises test your reading?						
Which exercises test your writing?						
How many marks can you get in each exercise?						
What is the word limit for longer written answers?						
Do you:						
• copy answers from the text?						
• write A, B, C or D?						
• tick boxes?						
• write your own answers?						

TIP

At the start of the exam, when the teacher says that you are allowed to open the question paper, always look quickly through the whole paper. This will allow you to plan how much time you should spend on each exercise/question.

CHECK YOUR PROGRESS

Was there anything you didn't know about the Reading and Writing exam? Now test yourself to see if you can remember everything mentioned in the two previous exercises.

Are the following statements true (T) or false (F)? Circle the correct letter for each statement.

1	There are eight parts in the Reading and Writing exam.	T / F
2	Your writing skills will be tested in two parts of the exam only.	T / F
3	You are given 2.5 hours to complete the whole Reading and Writing exam.	T / F
4	You will receive more marks for your answers in the writing part than in the reading part of the exam.	T / F
5	If you do not understand a word in the reading part, you can use a dictionary to find the meaning.	T / F
6	You have to answer all the questions in the reading part, but you can choose which writing question – Exercise 5 or Exercise 6 – you want to answer.	T / F
7	In Exercise 1, some questions may need more than one detail as your answer.	T / F
8	In Exercise 1, when you find the answer in the text, you should copy it as it is in the text. You do not need to change the answer in any way.	T / F
9	In Exercise 2, you have to match all the statements to the texts. There are no spare statements.	T / F
10	In Exercise 3, you only need to find one detail in the text to go under each heading.	T / F
11	In Exercise 3, you should paraphrase the answers that you find in the text.	T / F
12	In Exercise 4, you can tick more than one box for each answer.	T / F
13	In Exercises 5 and 6, students receive more marks for the language they use in their writing than for the content.	T / F
14	In Exercises 5 and 6, you can write as many words as you want as long as you answer the question.	T / F
15	In Exercise 5, students are sometimes asked to write a formal email (e.g. a complaint).	T / F
16	In Exercise 6, students have to write their answers in a more formal tone than in Exercise 5.	T / F
17	In Exercise 6, students always have to write a report.	T / F

Now go to the answer key for Section 1, Unit 1.1 and check your answers.

Your score: .... out of 17

Unit 1.2: Exam strategies

First, do the exercise in Test 1 as you would in the real exam. Then look at the **Reflection** section to see some useful guidance on how to do this type of exercise. Also, look at the **Learn from mistakes** section to see common mistakes made by other students. Finally, do the same type of exercise in Test 2 to see if you have improved.

Test 1

Exercise 1

Read the article about a modern art competition called the Turner Prize and then answer the questions.

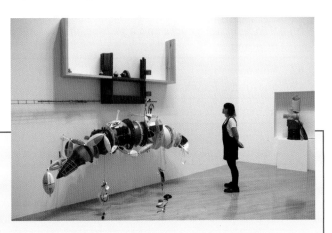

The Turner Prize

There are many arts competitions held globally, ranging from photography to sculpture. One of the most famous visual arts competitions in Europe is the Turner Prize, which has been held in Britain since 1984. It was originally the idea of a group called the Patrons of New Art. The group itself came together only two years before the first Turner Prize competition, in 1982. The founders wanted to make the public more interested in modern art and to obtain new artworks for the Tate Gallery in London.

The competition was named after William Turner, an English painter (1775–1851) who, like most artists of that time, focused on painting landscapes. His way of painting was seen as rather controversial by many of his contemporaries – something that did not go unnoticed by the founders of the competition when they were thinking about a name for the contest.

At the beginning of the competition, unlike today, anyone who made an impact in art could have been awarded the prize. This included managers of galleries, curators or art critics. The only restriction was that these people had to have been born live or work in Britain, which is still the case today. Each year, the judges choose the winner from four shortlisted artists. After the competition was founded, people disapproved of the absence of women on the shortlist, and it wasn't until 1987 that the first two female artists were finally shortlisted.

Apart from the prestige that winning this competition carries, there is also a financial award of £40,000, which is divided among all the finalists. The artist that comes first receives £25,000 and the other shortlisted artists get £5,000 each. The jury's decision about who the winner is has often been questioned by the public because not everybody sees the winning artwork as original or exciting. The critics also dislike the fact that the selection process isn't clear. The public's divided opinion over modern art led a group called the 'K foundation' to award an anti-Turner Prize to the worst artist in Britain. In 1994, this prize was given to an artist that also won the Turner Prize in 1993 for her sculpture called 'House'.

The finalists exhibit their artwork at an exhibition, which is traditionally hosted by the Tate Britain gallery in London. In the past, it was pointed out that there was a lack of space for the exhibits at this venue. So, every other year, since 2011, galleries situated in other British cities have been selected to host the Turner Prize. These cities include Glasgow, and more recently Coventry, but it was Liverpool where this tradition began in 2007. And this is also the only city, apart from London, that has hosted this competition more than once.

1 When did the competition first take place?

.... [1]

2 Why did the founders of the competition find Turner's paintings interesting?

.... [1]

3 How many artists are in the final stage of the competition?

.... [1]

4 How much money does the winner receive?

.... [1]

5 Where was the first Turner Prize competition held outside London?

.... [1]

6 What has the competition been criticised for? Give **three** details.

....

....

.... [3]

[Total: 8]

TIP

When you do Exercise 1, first answer Questions 1–5, then read the text again and find the answers to Question 6.

TIP

In Exercise 1, Questions 1–5 come in the same order as the answers in the text.

In this reading exercise, you get 1 mark for each correct answer you provide.

TIP

The last question in Exercise 1 always asks for **three** details and you get 3 marks for these. The answers are found throughout the text. There might be more than three details in the text. However, you only need to include three in your answer. You will not receive extra marks for giving more than that.

TIP

If you are unsure about some of your answers, put a question mark next to these and have a look at them again once you have completed the whole exercise. However, do not spend too long on questions you do not know how to answer. If you do, you might not have enough time to complete other exercises in the rest of the paper.

When you have finished doing this part of the test, go to the answer key for Section 1, Unit 1.2 and check your answers.

Your score:..................... out of 8

Reflection

Now think about the way you did Test 1, Exercise 1. Read the questions in the following table and put YES or NO to show you have, or have not, done these things. The questions remind you about the things you should do in Exercise 1 in the Reading and Writing exam. If some of your answers are NO, these are the areas you need to practise a bit more to improve your performance in the exam.

Before you started reading	YES or NO	Guidance
1 Did you read the questions first before reading the text?		Read the questions first. You need to know what details to look for before you start reading. You should: • look at Question 1 • read the text • find the answer to Question 1 • highlight the answer in the text • write your answer on the line provided. Then do the same for Questions 2–5, continuing reading from where you left off. Remember you will need to read the whole text again for Question 6.
2 Did you highlight the important words in each question?		Highlight important words in the question to remind you what detail you are looking for (e.g. the year of the first competition).
While you were reading	**YES or NO**	**Guidance**
3 Did you underline the answers when you found them in the text?		Sometimes you need to look at the text again to check that you have selected the correct detail. It is easier to check your answers if you underline them in the text. If you do not underline your answers, you might have to read some parts of the text again and waste your time during the exam.
4 Did you transfer your answers from the text onto the line provided as it is written in the text?		In Exercise 1, when you transfer your answers, you should use the same words as in the text. You do not need to change the wording of the answer. If you try to paraphrase the answer, you might change the meaning and lose marks.
5 Did you transfer the necessary details only, not the whole sentence or irrelevant information?		In this exercise, you are tested on your ability to select the correct detail when reading. You are not showing this skill if you copy the whole sentence. By writing too much, you also waste your time in the exam.
6 Did you check that you did not select any distracting information as part of your answer?		If you include a distracting detail together with a correct detail, the whole answer would be wrong and would not be given any marks.
7 Did you answer Questions 1–5 first and then scan the text to find the answers to Question 6?		It is very difficult to find the answers to Question 6 while you are answering Questions 1–5. It is easier to read the text again after you have answered Questions 1–5. You can scan read the text much more quickly the second time and focus on the three details.

After you finished reading	YES or NO	Guidance
8 Did you check that you included the correct type of detail required for each question (e.g. a number, a name)?		

If you answered 'No' to any of the questions in the **Reflection** section, try to follow all the guidance from this section when you do Test 2, Exercise 1.

Learn from mistakes

Before you do Test 2, Exercise 1, look at the following exercise. It includes some students' answers to Test 1, Exercise 1. What did the students do wrong?

1	Before answering Question 1	When <u>did</u> the competition first take place?

2	Answer to Question 1	1982

3	Answer to Question 2	Turner was an English painter. He was born in 1775 and died in 1851.

4	Answer to Question 2	No-one painted like him.

5	Answer to Question 3	for artists

6	Answer to Question 3	There are four artists in the final stage of the competition.

7	Answer to Question 4	$250,000

8	Answer to Question 4	(£40,000) £25,000

9	Answer to Question 5	Glasgow, Coventry and Liverpool

10	Answer to Question 5	2007

TIP

After you check your answers, it is very important to look at your own mistakes. Think about why you made those mistakes to make sure you do not repeat them in the future. If you never look at your mistakes, you will not improve.

11	Answer to Question 6	absence of women, jury's decision the selection process, a lack of space

12	Answer to Question 6	jury process space

Now do Test 2, Exercise 1, and remember to follow all the guidance from the **Reflection** section for Test 1.

Test 2

Exercise 1

Read the article about a dinosaur called the Archaeopteryx and then answer the questions.

Is Archaeopteryx the birds' direct ancestor?

We learn at school that dinosaurs walked the Earth for 165 million years until they became extinct – something scientists believe was mainly caused by an asteroid crashing into our planet about 65 million years ago. However, it's less well known that one group of dinosaurs survived, including the Archaeopteryx, which was half dinosaur, half bird.

In 1860, scientists first found a fossilised feather that may have come from the Archaeopteryx dinosaur. This was followed by a more exciting find, in 1861, when the first bones of the Archaeopteryx were discovered. Just over a decade later, in 1874, a farmer discovered some more bones, which later turned out to be an even more complete skeleton of the Archaeopteryx dinosaur than the initial one.

All three finds were made in Germany and it is also where the complete skeleton can be seen – in the Humboldt Museum in Berlin. The dinosaur was given the name Archaeopteryx, which originates from the old Greek words for *ancient* and *feather*. It is also sometimes referred to by its German name *Urvogel*, which means *first bird*.

Scientists noticed that, apart from the usual features expected in these types of dinosaurs, like teeth, claws or a long bony tail, the fossils of Archaeopteryx also showed marks that resembled feathers, which was really fascinating for the scientific community. Scientists started to think that this dinosaur might have been a link between dinosaurs and birds. However, this dinosaur had a long way to go before it would look like the birds we know nowadays. The question was, though, what Archaeopteryx needed feathers for if it wasn't for flying. The most obvious reason would be for body temperature control. It is also possible that their feathers played a role in their communication with each other.

Archaeopteryx wasn't a large dinosaur compared to other, much larger ones, which could be as heavy as 14 African elephants put together. With its 1 kilogram of weight and body length of 50 centimetres, Archaeopteryx wasn't much bigger than a pigeon. And, just like these birds, Archaeopteryx probably exploited its feathers to attract females.

Scientists don't know a lot about Archaeopteryx's diet, but they believe it mainly consisted of small reptiles. It is also believed to have occasionally replaced these with small mammals or even insects.

Despite having feathers, Archaeopteryx did not fly in the sky, but some scientists think that the dinosaur attempted very short flights near the ground when it needed to hunt or escape danger. And it must have been in situations like these when the feathers helped to ensure it remained hidden when it needed to. However, before dinosaurs could fully take to the sky, they still had to develop a few more features.

1   When was the first skeleton of the Archaeopteryx dinosaur found?

.... [1]

2   What does the German name for this dinosaur mean?

.... [1]

3   What did scientists find interesting about the Archaeopteryx's fossils?

.... [1]

4   What is the size of Archaeopteryx's body compared to?

.... [1]

5   What did Archaeopteryx eat most of the time?

.... [1]

6   What did Archaeopteryx use feathers for? Give **three** details.

....

....

.... [3]

[Total: 8]

When you have finished doing this part of the test, go to the answer key for Section 1, Unit 1.2 and check your answers.

Your score:..................... out of 8

CHECK YOUR PROGRESS

Now think about your progress so far and answer the following questions:

- Was your score in Test 2, Exercise 1 higher than in Test 1, or not? Why do you think this is?
- After doing the **Reflection** section for this part of the exam, did you find it easier to do Test 2? What tips did you find helpful?
- Is there anything you still find difficult? What are you going to do to improve this?

TIP

It is important to reflect on your own progress. This will help you identify which areas are your strengths or weaknesses. If you can identify your weaknesses, you will then know what you need to revise more before the exam. The **Check your progress** sections, and the **Progress chart** at the beginning of the book will help you to do that.

Develop your skills

In Exercise 1, you are tested on whether you can select the correct details and understand the connection between them in a longer piece of text. These texts can be taken from leaflets, magazine articles or from a website, etc.

Try some of the following to improve your skills in reading for detail:

- Select a short piece of text (leaflets or blogs are the best for this activity) and make a list of some question words (e.g. *who, when, what, how often, how much*). Then scan read the text and see how many answers you can find.

- Select an article and highlight random nouns, names or numbers in the text (e.g. *28%, John Burnes, Victoria Square, in January*). Then read the text around these details and find out what they refer to (e.g. *the price of houses has risen by 28%*).

- To practise your scan reading for detail, use materials like leaflets, TV guides, cinema programmes, etc. For example, you could scan read a TV guide and find how many, and what, films are being shown on one evening. You can scan read cinema programmes to try and find out if there are any comedy films and what time they are shown, etc.

- In the exam you are not allowed to use a dictionary. That is why it is important that you learn to guess the meaning of unknown vocabulary from the context when you are reading. Choose a short newspaper article, then scan it and underline all the words that you do not understand. Then read the text around each word and look for clues that might help you guess the meaning. When you have finished, check the meaning in an English dictionary to see if you were right.

Test 1

Exercise 2

Read the article about four students (**A–D**) and their experience of studying. Then answer Question **7**.

Experience of studying

Four students share their thoughts about studying

A   Hoda

My favourite subjects at school are languages. I'm studying French, Russian and English because I'm hoping to become an interpreter. However, I don't have the same interest in subjects that involve practical experiments. This doesn't mean, though, that I neglect my homework for these subjects. I always try my best at whatever I do. That's why I like my tutor, who's very experienced. He shows me how to do things properly so that I don't pick up any bad habits. When I started learning French, the pronunciation was very tricky, but with practice it improved and now, everyone comments on how good my accent is. I've also learnt that there are more ways of studying things during the lesson. At the moment, I like when the teacher asks us to put words into categories and use pictures to memorise new vocabulary. My friend, on the other hand, prefers writing down definitions from the dictionary, but I see very little value in this.

B   Kim

I've recently changed schools, so I haven't fully settled in yet. It takes some time to get to know a new place, but the teachers have been very welcoming. They say I'm doing rather well and won't need any extra tuition to catch up with the others. I'm really happy when we're encouraged to work in groups. Not only does this give me a chance to meet new classmates, but we also think of interesting ideas together, so it's easier to complete the tasks we're given. The only thing I find quite demanding is the timetable. Twice a week, my lessons finish very late, which is exhausting. Then, when I get home, doing homework is a real challenge, but I noticed that if I get up before everybody else does, I get a lot of schoolwork done then. But I still have to remember to leave enough time to help my younger brother to get ready for school.

C   Kinga

I'm in my final year of college and planning to start a law degree at university next year. Getting ready for this involves a lot of research and I'd be lost if I couldn't access all the resources available online. Some of my school friends go to revision study groups in the afternoon. I've tried these groups a few times because I'm rather behind with my maths. At first, they seemed OK, but then I got frustrated with some of the people there who just wanted to chat, so we never got any work done. That's when my friend agreed, after I managed to persuade her, to support me with my maths studies. I'm not doing that badly in other

subjects, so I'm better off just doing some self-study when necessary. So, that's what I like to do in the school library these days, straight after my classes. While I'm there, I can also read about other things that interest me.

D   Miguel

When I was younger, I got into all sorts of trouble at school. I tended to disrupt the class a lot by making other students laugh or asking the teacher silly questions. My parents didn't know what to do with me. After school, I would spend lots of time online doing everything but my homework. Then I started a new school and got more involved in my studies. There was so much more to do and there still is, so, to cope with the amount of information, I take notes in the lessons, which I couldn't do without when it comes to my revision. Even some of my classmates have asked for my notes after their own approaches to revising have failed them. Recently, I got into science. Sometimes we go on trips and we learn about real science in everyday life. It's a shame that we don't do more things like this in other subjects.

For each statement, write the correct letter A, B, C or D on the line.

Question 7

Which person gives the following information?

a   the idea that it is important to learn with a good teacher   .... [1]

b   a preference for studying with other students   .... [1]

c   a claim that writing things down is really helpful for them   .... [1]

d   an idea of how much the writer relies on technology   .... [1]

e   a preference for studying early in the day   .... [1]

f   an understanding that made the writer get help from someone   .... [1]

g   the fact that doing extra work after school is a positive experience   .... [1]

h   a wish to have more practical school lessons   .... [1]

i   a description of different classroom activities to help learning   .... [1]

[Total: 9]

When you have finished doing this part of the test, go to the answer key for Section 1, Unit 1.2 and check your answers.

Your score:........................ out of 9

Reflection

Now think about the way you did Test 1, Exercise 2. Read the questions in the table and put YES or NO to show you have, or have not, done these things. The questions remind you about the things you should do in Exercise 2 in the Reading and Writing exam. If some of your answers are NO, these are the areas you need to practise a bit more to improve your performance in the exam.

Before you started reading	YES or NO	Guidance
1 Did you read the opinions (a)–(i) before reading the article?		The opinions can sometimes be noun phrases (e.g. a suggestion of how to deal with a difficult situation) but they can also be written as questions (e.g. which person suggests a way of dealing with a difficult situation).
2 Did you highlight the important words in each opinion?		Highlighting important words will remind you what detail you are looking for (e.g. *good teacher* and *important*). Remember that the vocabulary used in the opinions is not always the same as the vocabulary used in the text. The ideas in the text are often paraphrased and implied.
While you were reading	**YES or NO**	**Guidance**
3 Did you read each text one at a time?		Read one text at a time. Then select all the opinions from the list that this text expresses before you move on to the next text. The order of the opinions on the list is usually different from the order they appear in the text.
4 Did you underline the answers when you found them in each text?		Check that the opinion you find in the text fully matches the idea in the opinion from the list. If only part of the idea is the same, it might not be the correct answer, but a wrong distracting detail. If you underline the ideas in the text, it will be easier for you to check them against the opinions from the list.
After you finished reading	**YES or NO**	**Guidance**
5 Did you match all the opinions (a)–(i) from the list to one of the texts?		Do not leave any spaces blank. If you do not know the answer, guess it. You will not lose marks for wrong answers. There are no extra opinions on the list. This means that you should use all the opinions (a)–(i) in your answers.

6	Did you check again the answers you weren't sure about the first time?		If you are not sure about some of your answers, or you cannot decide between two opinions, while you are doing the exercise, put a question mark next to them. When you finish doing the whole exercise, go back to these answers to check them again and make your final decision about what the answer should be.
7	Did you write only one letter per line for each opinion?		Do not include more than one answer. If you change your mind, you need to cross out your first attempt and write your final answer clearly next to it. Do not overwrite your first attempt, as answers like these may not be legible and you may lose marks.

If you answered 'No' to any of the questions in the **Reflection** section, try to follow all the guidance from this section when you do Test 2, Exercise 2.

Learn from mistakes

Before you do Test 2, Exercise 2, look at the following exercise. It includes some students' answers to Test 1, Exercise 2. What did the students do wrong?

1	Answer to Question 7a	the idea that it is important to learn with a good teacher ....A/C........

2	Answer to Question 7b	preference for studying with other students ....B........

3	Answer to Question 7c	a claim that writing things down is really helpful for them ....

4	Answer to Question 7d	an idea of how much the writer relies on technology ....Kinga........

Now do Test 2, Exercise 2, and remember to follow all the guidance from the **Reflection** section for Test 1.

Test 2

Exercise 2

Read the article about four people (**A**–**D**) and what they say about their jobs.
Then answer Question **7**.

Are you happy in your job?

Four people share their thoughts about jobs.

A   Alice

I've been working for a major publishing company for over a decade now. When I started, I had to work very hard to get noticed. I wasn't necessarily trying to get a higher position, but I wanted my manager to see I could be relied on. With time I was asked if I'd be interested in being in charge of some projects. It's all the opportunities I'm given that make my job so interesting. The only downside of my work is how long it takes to get there in the morning. Some days I get stuck in traffic, which wastes a lot of time. That's why I recently requested if I could do some of my work from home and, to my surprise, my boss agreed. I actually get more things done this way compared to the days in the office. I suppose this is also a good way to avoid listening to other colleagues arguing about things.

B   Bruno

I teach history at a college near my house. In this respect I'm lucky – I can avoid the morning traffic jams because I walk to college. The working week goes by very quickly for me because I really enjoy my job, but there is no denying that teaching doesn't suit everybody. Without enough patience and love for this job, some people decide to leave and look for a completely different job after just a year or two. I admit it might have crossed my mind a few times when I was a newly qualified teacher, but not anymore. What makes me sad though is when a good teacher leaves because of financial reasons. Teachers are hard-working people and deserve a pay rise. The school where I work is relatively modern and has a fantastic library and gym, which my colleagues and I can use in the evening after long hours of teaching.

C   Celine

I trained as a chef five years ago. I thought this would be my ideal job because I've always enjoyed cooking and being responsible for big family dinners. However, I've come to the conclusion that, while I enjoy cooking for my family, I don't want to do this for a living. Plus, I can't see myself being promoted any time soon either. Having said that, the restaurant where I work has the latest equipment, so this makes all the difference. I have no complaints about that, but the same can't be said about the schedule. I'm an early bird so I tend to wind down in the evening, but that's the time when the restaurant kitchen gets the busiest. The team are very friendly on the whole and I've made some friends there. Although, I feel that one of the supervisors often unfairly criticises me for all sorts of little things.

D   Daniel

Two years ago, I took on a job for a large company dealing with computers. I used to dream of running my own company, but I've come to realise that it'd take a lot of savings to do this – something that I don't quite have yet. I also feel I still have a lot to learn and that is why my new role was totally unexpected. I'm now managing a team of five people and couldn't be happier. My family often complains about my long hours and the fact that I'm not at home with them enough. Quite a few meetings I have to attend are held abroad. My son thinks it's quite exciting, and doesn't believe me when I tell him there are so many things that need doing, like giving presentations, making new contacts, that hardly any time is left for sightseeing. However, I always make it up to my family during our holidays.

For each question, write the correct letter A, B, C or D on the line.

Question 7

Which person…

a   suggests that people in this job are underpaid?   .... [1]

b   is thinking of a career change?   .... [1]

c   is surprised by their recent promotion?   .... [1]

d   doesn't get on with one of the staff?   .... [1]

e   feels that the working hours don't suit them?   .... [1]

f   thinks that people doing this job need to have certain qualities?   .... [1]

g   enjoys the variety of responsibilities their job offers?   .... [1]

h   says the job involves a lot of travelling?   .... [1]

i   doesn't have to travel to work every day?   .... [1]

[Total: 9]

When you have finished doing this part of the test, go to the answer key for Section 1, Unit 1.2 and check your answers.

Your score:...................... out of 9

CHECK YOUR PROGRESS

Now think about your progress so far and answer the following questions:

*   Was your score in Test 2, Exercise 2, higher than in Test 1, or not? Why do you think this is?

*   After doing the **Reflection** section for this part of the exam, did you find it easier to do Test 2? What guidance did you find helpful?

*   Is there anything you still find difficult? What are you going to do to improve this?

Develop your skills

In Exercise 2, you are tested on whether you can select the correct ideas/opinions and understand the connections between them. The ideas and opinions are either directly stated or implied, which means not stated directly.

Try the following activity to improve these reading skills:

*   Try to read a range of texts where the author expresses their opinions (e.g. film/play/video game reviews, customer reviews online about various products and services, blogs).

*   Find what the writer is writing about (e.g. a film review – acting, directing, screenplay) and what the writer's opinion is (i.e. positive, negative or mixed).

*   Read the text again and find exactly what the writer liked or did not like and the reasons for their opinions.

*   Then find the phrases that the writer uses to express their opinions (e.g. it was a complete let-down, it did not come up to our expectations, it is one of a kind).

*   Finally, think of different ways of saying the same thing – try to paraphrase the same idea by using similar phrases. This will also help you improve your writing skills.

Test 1

Exercise 3

Read the article about CYTECH, a company that designs wearable technology for cyclists, and then complete the notes.

CYTECH – wearable technology for cyclists

CYTECH, which stands for cycling and technology, is a relatively young company, but it has already found a place in the market of wearable technology. The founder, Jessica Curtis, set up this new company to combine her two biggest passions in life: cycling and designing.

Jessica first presented her plans to a friend of hers who specialises in the production of LED lighting, which is a type of low-energy lighting. Together they came up with a new design of clothing for cyclists.

Since then, Jessica has been getting feedback from her friends, who are mostly young professionals. They tend to cycle to work and often complained that they couldn't find a visibility jacket that would be functional but at the same time looked attractive. And that is exactly what Jessica has achieved with her latest clothing line for cyclists, which consists of jackets, hats and trousers. It is surprising that, in this day and age, most manufacturers of wearable technology don't focus on clothing for cyclists, but on gadgets, like smartwatches, instead. And that's exactly what Jessica's intention was – to fill a gap in the market.

Another unique feature, which is proving a huge hit with the wearers, is that the LED lighting used on these items is well hidden. Most cyclists also appreciate the fact that the battery life of this lighting is about 14 hours, which is really impressive, especially when compared to how long the average smartphone battery lasts.

In recent years, we have seen a significant increase in people taking up cycling, not only for their own pleasure, but also as a more reliable and environmentally friendly means of transport in cities around the world. The rise in cyclists on the road has brought the need to improve road safety more into the spotlight. This was something that also played a vital role in Jessica's decision to go into this business. When the clothing itself was tested, it was visible as far as 400 metres away – something Jessica was particularly pleased with.

The fabric that is used to make these clothes is both waterproof and machine washable – two practical facts that certainly can't be overlooked.

Currently, Jessica is looking into working with energy-harvesting fabrics next. Energy harvesting is a way of storing power from external sources like the wind or the sun and then using the small sources of energy for everyday purposes, such as charging your smartphone or any other portable electronic devices.

Jessica has become a role model for other aspiring entrepreneurs and is often asked what the secret of her success is. She believes that there is no harm in aiming high, but urges anyone who wants to follow in her footsteps to invest in thorough market research. The bottom line is – the customer comes first.

Imagine you are going to give a talk about the CYTECH company and their products to your classmates. Use words from the article to help you write some notes.

Make short notes under each heading.

8   Reasons why Jessica started designing clothing for cyclists

    • ....

    • .... [2]

9 Benefits of CYTECH products

Example: functional

- ....

- ....

- ....

- ....

- .... [5]

[Total: 7]

> When you have finished doing this part of the test, go to the answer key for Section 1, Unit 1.2 and check your answers.
>
> Your score:..................... out of 7

Reflection

Now think about the way you did Test 1, Exercise 3. Read the questions in the following table and put YES or NO to show you have, or have not, done these things. The questions remind you about the things you should do in Exercise 3 in the Reading exam. If some of your answers are NO, these are the areas you need to practise a bit more to improve your performance in the Reading exam.

Before you started reading	YES or NO	Guidance
1 Did you first carefully read the instructions and the headings for your notes?		The order of the headings for your notes may not always be the same as the order of the ideas in the text. Also, the ideas in the text may not always come in the same paragraph. They are often spread throughout the text.
2 Did you highlight the important words in each heading?		Highlight important words in the question to remind you what detail you are looking for (e.g. *reasons* and *starting*). It is a good idea to use a different highlighter pen for each heading and then to use the same colour to underline the ideas in the text.
While you were reading	YES or NO	Guidance
3 Did you highlight the details/ ideas in the text that are required for each heading?		Read the text and highlight all the examples required for the first heading. Then transfer the correct number of examples onto the lines provided under the first heading. Repeat the same for the second heading, and so on.
4 Did you transfer the ideas under the correct heading, on the lines provided?		If you highlight ideas that go under the same heading with a different colour highlighter, it will be easier for you to see which ideas should go under the same heading. Also make sure that each idea is written on a separate line.

While you were reading	YES or NO	Guidance
5 Did you transfer the answers as they are worded in the text?		Do not paraphrase your answers. You are tested on whether you can find the correct details. By changing the wording of the answer, you might also change the meaning and lose marks. Use the same wording as in the text.
After you finished reading	**YES or NO**	**Guidance**
6 Did you include the correct number of details under each heading?		The number of marks shown under each heading tells you how many ideas are required. You get one mark for each correct idea. There are usually more ideas in the text than you need.
7 Did you check that you did not include the same idea twice?		Sometimes there may be two details that talk about the same idea. If you include both of these similar ideas as two separate answers, you will only get one mark. For example, *the battery life of this lighting is about 14 hours* and *[14 hours of battery life] is really impressive* both express the same benefit of CYTECH products and should only be included once.
8 Did you check that you included the details under the correct heading?		If you include the correct detail, but write it under the wrong heading, this detail will not receive a mark.

If you answered 'No' to any of the questions in the **Reflection** section, try to follow all the guidance from this section when you do Test 2, Exercise 3.

Learn from mistakes

Before you do Test 2, Exercise 3, look at the following exercise. It includes some students' answers to Test 1, Exercise 3. What did the students do wrong?

1	Answer to Question 8	• improve roads • she is a designer

2	Answer to Question 8	• CYTECH, which stands for cycling and technology, is a relatively young company, but it has already found a place in the market of wearable technology. The founder, Jessica Curtis, set up this new company to combine her two biggest passions in life: cycling and designing.

3	Answer to Question 9	• fill a gap in the market

4	Answer to Question 9	• attractive • machine washable • waterproof • stores power from the sun • ....
5	Answer to Question 9	• the LED lighting cannot be accessed by other people
6	Answer to Question 9	• (charge phone) / machine washable / waterproof / attractive / LED lighting hidden • .... • .... • .... • ....

Now do Test 2, Exercise 3, and remember to follow all the guidance from the **Reflection** section for Test 1.

Test 2

Exercise 3

Read the article about how to become an astronaut and then complete the notes.

Could you be a future astronaut?

Becoming an astronaut has always been a dream of many young boys and girls, but the question is – how do you become one?

The NTV television channel is launching a reality series that may help to answer this question. It will offer people who think they have what it takes to become an astronaut the opportunity to try out what it is really like to go through a selection process and a space preparation programme. The TV channel has asked a former astronaut who also used to be in charge of the International Space Station (ISS) to oversee this process to make sure it is as close to the real thing as possible. 'Unless you have self-discipline, you shouldn't even think of handing in your application.' The real process

is very demanding, both physically and mentally, so hopeful applicants won't make it without enough determination.

People who have been selected to go to space and to work at the ISS have come from varied backgrounds. At the beginning of space exploration, astronauts often came from an army background, for example army pilots. These days, successful applicants usually have some previous experience in science and engineering, which is an advantage and certainly helps with the scientific experiments that are carried out by the crew of each space mission. These can range from examining cosmic dust to growing lettuce.

The space programme is also suited to people who are good at staying calm under pressure, especially when they have to deal with zero gravity once on board the ISS. This is the lack of the force that pulls objects to the ground, something we experience on Earth, but not in space. This means that all objects float around the space station and can potentially be a danger to the astronauts. Because of this, astronauts need to predict in which direction the objects are likely to move. People who apply are, therefore, tested on their spatial awareness. Even though research has shown that this is something that

can be taught, it's preferable for successful applicants to already possess this quality. The tough selection process is absolutely necessary to prepare them for what lies ahead, where working together as a team will prove essential.

To many, being at the ISS might sound like a lot of fun, but this is not always the case. One of the downsides, for example, is the loss of muscle and bone mass after spending time in space. On return to Earth, it takes astronauts some time to get back to normal and regain their strength. And that's why a good level of general physical health is expected at the initial stage of the process.

The reality show starts on 3 March, but if you think you have what it takes already, you can try applying directly to the ISS.

Imagine you are going to give a talk about how to become an astronaut to your science class at school. Use words from the article to help you write some notes.

Make short notes under each heading.

8   Skills and personal qualities needed to become an astronaut

   Example: self-discipline

   - ....
   - ....
   - ....
   - .... [4]

9   What is expected of all astronauts while they are in space

   - ....
   - ....
   - .... [3]

[Total: 7]

When you have finished doing this part of the test, go to the answer key for Section 1, Unit 1.2 and check your answers.

Your score:...................... out of 7

CHECK YOUR PROGRESS

Now think about your progress so far and answer the following questions:

- Was your score in Test 2, Exercise 3 higher than in Test 1? Why do you think this is?

- After doing the **Reflection** section for this part of the exam, did you find it easier to do Test 2? What guidance did you find helpful?

- Is there anything you still find difficult? What are you going to do to improve this?

Develop your skills

In Exercise 3, you are tested on whether you can select the correct details and ideas/opinions and understand the connections between these ideas.

Try the following activity to improve these reading skills:

- Try to read a range of texts where the author writes about advantages and disadvantages, success and failure, benefits and difficulties, etc. You might find these ideas in texts like travel blogs, online articles about various projects or magazine articles about history/nature/science. Do not choose articles that are too long. The articles you choose should be of a similar length to the articles in the real exam – approximately one A4 page.

- First, quickly skim the text to get the general idea and see whether it contains ideas like reasons, results, pros/cons, etc.

- Select one of the ideas (e.g. reasons), scan read the text again and find examples of reasons. Ignore all the other information.

- When you get better at these reading skills, time yourself each time you read a new article to see if your reading speed is improving too.

Test 1

Exercise 4

Read the blog written by someone who films wildlife in different parts of the world, and then answer the questions.

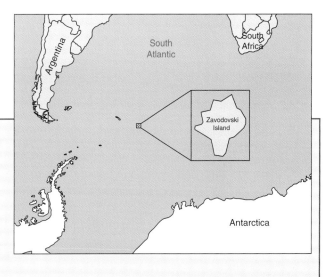

Filming penguins on Zavodovski Island

Today we're leaving Zavodovski Island, where we've spent several weeks filming penguins. This island in the South Atlantic Ocean is uninhabited and hosts the largest penguin colony in the world. The species that lives on this island is called the chinstrap penguin, named after the black line that runs from ear to ear underneath its beak. The island is located in such extreme conditions that life for the penguins here is very dangerous. While there are plenty of fish in the ocean surrounding the island, getting to it is not an easy task. The waves are huge and smash against the rocks with great power.

Our whole team spent several weeks preparing for this expedition. We took this stage very seriously. After all, getting ready for filming in a very remote region isn't the same as packing for a couple of weeks' family holidays with all the conveniences of the modern world. Apart from the usual precautions like making sure we had enough food, the appropriate equipment and clothing, we also gave a lot of thought to safety. We had to have everything ready in case of a medical emergency. All of this is probably what anyone would expect to happen before setting off on an expedition. The environmental impact the team may have on the island and its wildlife is one aspect that doesn't cross many people's minds though. We were very lucky to benefit from the experience, and knowledge, of Pete Johansson, who was in charge of our expedition. He made sure we knew exactly what to do to minimise our impact. This included vacuuming the inside of our backpacks and cleaning our shoes to avoid bringing any seeds to the island, and potentially causing harm to the local environment.

On the day we got to the island, the sea was very rough. This made getting the filming gear onto dry land no easy task. And, as if that wasn't hard enough, pulling it up a cliff to the exact location really tested us to the limit. The weather can change very quickly in this region, as we soon discovered, which made filming rather tricky at times. We couldn't stay on one spot for too long because of the strong, biting winds, so we had to do everything very quickly. But you realise it's all well worth it when you see the penguins. They resemble funny little people in dinner jackets. I could watch them forever swaying from one side to another as they walk around the island. And they're very curious too, which meant they interfered with us setting up the filming equipment.

These friendly creatures, who are more than half a metre tall, now dominate the island. They build their nests here and have their chicks. The nest is round and made from collected stones, which aren't in short supply on the island. Both parents take *it* in turns to sit on the eggs to keep them warm until the chicks are ready to come out, after about 37 days. The chicks don't leave the nests for another few weeks, when they join the penguin 'nursery', where they're looked after together with all the other youngsters.

Now that it's time to leave, saying our goodbyes isn't proving nearly as easy as we thought it would because we've certainly grown close to the penguins. Our cameraman even has his favourite ones and has given each of them a name. It's been a true privilege to film these amazing animals in their natural habit and witness some of the key moments in their everyday lives.

47

10 In paragraph 1, we learn that

A Zavodovski Island is the only place where chinstrap penguins are found. ☐

B Nobody had been to the island before the film crew arrived. ☐

C The environment on the island is challenging for the penguins. ☐

[1]

11 What does the writer suggest about the preparation stage of the expedition?

A He would rather have been getting ready for a holiday with his family. ☐

B He appreciated there was someone who was very experienced on the team. ☐

C He was surprised by the number of things to consider before setting off. ☐

[1]

12 What did the filming crew find most difficult when they arrived at the island?

A the mountainous landscape ☐

B the unpredictable weather ☐

C the sea storm ☐

[1]

13 In paragraph 3, the writer mentions 'dinner jackets' to demonstrate

   A how formal the penguins' way of walking is. ☐

   B how similar the penguins' behaviour is to humans. ☐

   C how amusing the penguins' appearance is. ☐

    [1]

14 In paragraph 4, what activity does 'it' refer to?

   A building their nests ☐

   B looking after the eggs ☐

   C collecting stones ☐

    [1]

15 What was the writer's main reason for writing this blog?

   A To raise awareness of the environmental changes on the island. ☐

   B To advise people visiting the island about how to prepare for the trip. ☐

   C To describe how satisfying a wildlife expedition can be. ☐

    [1]

    [Total: 6]

When you have finished doing this part of the test, go to the answer key for Section 1, Unit 1.2 and check your answers.

Your score: .... out of 6

Reflection

Now think about the way you did Test 1, Exercise 4. Read the questions in the following table and put YES or NO to show you have, or have not, done these things. The questions remind you about the things you should do in Exercise 4 in the Reading and Writing exam. If some of your answers are NO, these are the areas you need to practise a bit more to improve your performance in the exam.

Before you started reading	YES or NO	Guidance
1 Did you read the questions before reading the text?		The order of the questions is the same as the order of the answers in the text.
2 Did you highlight the important words in each question?		Only highlight the key words in the question, not in the options. The highlighted words will help you to locate the part of the text where the answer is more quickly. For example, some questions will tell you which paragraph you need to look at to find the answer.

Before you started reading	YES or NO	Guidance
3 Did you check which questions focus on referencing words or vocabulary phrases?		To locate the answers to questions that test referencing words or vocabulary phrases, you are given the number of the line where the word or phrase appears in the text. This means you can locate the correct part of the text very quickly.
4 Did you check if any of the questions are 'global' questions (e.g. the main reason/purpose the text was written)?		Always check if there is a 'global' question. This type of question may not always be included in Exercise 4. But, when it is, remember that you will have to read the whole text to be able to answer this question. Such questions may focus on: • the main purpose of the text (e.g. to entertain, to inform, to encourage) • what the whole text describes (e.g. an experience, challenges) • what the writer suggests in the whole text (e.g. a change is needed, an idea that is often misunderstood)
While you were reading	**YES or NO**	**Guidance**
5 Did you read the text quickly to find the part of the text where the answer is located for each question?		Remember that for some questions you are given the number of the line in the text so that you can locate the answers more quickly.
6 Did you read the part of the text with the answer in more slowly and match it to the correct option, A–C?		It is a good idea to highlight the answers in the text when you find them. You can then always go back to this part of the text if you need to check anything. Look at the highlighted text and make sure the idea matches the option completely. If it does not, this means it is probably a distracting detail and, therefore, not the correct answer. If you still cannot decide between two options, put a question mark next to this question and go back to it when you have finished the rest of the questions. If you are still not sure what the correct answer is, guess and put a tick in one of the boxes. Do not spend too long on one particular question, as you might run out of time.
7 Did you read the sentence before and after the sentence with the referencing word, or a phrase, in it?		Reference questions test your knowledge of referencing words (e.g. *it, this, them, those*). This type of question can also test how well you can guess the meaning of an unknown phrase, like idioms (e.g. *with flying colours, when the penny dropped, at the deep end*). To answer these questions, you will have to look for clues in the sentences that come before and after to be able decide what the meaning of these words/phrases is.

8	Did you read the text quickly again before answering the 'global' question?		You need to make sure that the idea in the option you select as your answer is an idea that is present in the whole text. If the idea is only present in one of the paragraphs, this means it is not the correct answer, but a distracting detail.
After you finished reading		**YES or NO**	**Guidance**
9	Did you tick one box for each question?		You should only tick one box for each question as there is only one correct answer for each question. The other two options are distracting details that are wrong.

If you answered 'No' to any of the questions in the **Reflection** section, try to follow all the guidance from this section when you do Test 2, Exercise 4.

Learn from mistakes

Before you do Test 2, Exercise 4, look at the following exercise. It includes some students' answers to Question 10 in Test 1, Exercise 4. What did the students do wrong?

1	In paragraph 1, we learn that	A	Zavodovski Island is the only place where chinstrap penguins are found.	☐
		B	Nobody had been to the island before the film crew arrived.	✔
		C	The environment on the island is challenging for the penguins.	✔

2	In paragraph 1, we learn that	A	Zavodovski Island is the only place where chinstrap penguins are found.	☐
		B	Nobody had been to the island before the film crew arrived.	☐
		C	The environment on the island is challenging for the penguins.	C

3	In paragraph 1, we learn that	A	Zavodovski Island is the only place where chinstrap penguins are found.	☐
		B	Nobody had been to the island before the film crew arrived.	☐
		Ⓒ	The environment on the island is challenging for the penguins.	☐

In paragraph 1, we learn that	A	Zavodovski Island is the only place where chinstrap penguins are found.	☐
	B	Nobody had been to the island before the film crew arrived.	☐
	C	The environment on the island is challenging for the penguins.	☐

Now do Test 2, Exercise 4, and remember to follow all the guidance from the **Reflection** section for Test 1.

Test 2

Exercise 4

Read the following blog written by Elisa Davies, who participated in a reality TV show about life in 19th-century London, and then answer the questions.

Life in 19th-century London

When I agreed to take part in this reality show about life in 19th-century London, I thought it'd just be a bit of fun – I couldn't have been more wrong. When I told my friends about my plans a few days before the filming started, they were all horrified. They couldn't understand why I'd put myself through such a process. I even had my mum crying on the phone to me. I think she had the image of reality shows where participants are made to do things to look silly. But it wasn't that kind of show. I knew that much.

The producers of the series took great care to recreate every single detail of what life was like in 19th-century London. For three weeks, we had to do everything that the people back then would have done. The first days were really hard. We were a group of 21st-century people and looking back we took a lot of things, like running water, for granted. You don't know what you've got until it's taken away from you.

We had to try hard to earn a living through selling things we made, for example, clothes or candles. I was given the task of sewing clothes, which we then sold at the local market. I'd never made clothes before, but to be able to earn money for food, I had to learn very quickly. To learn to sew, you need patience and practice – neither of which I had. I remember one day I'd been sewing for several hours, working on a shirt. My back was hurting from sitting in one position for too long, but I just kept going. This wasn't just for me, the whole group depended on me. If I hadn't completed sewing all the clothes, we wouldn't have had enough money for our dinner and rent. At the end of the day, when we were all sitting round the table eating, I was really proud of myself – a feeling I hadn't felt in a long time.

The house we were staying in was built in 1877. At that time, safety for the residents couldn't be guaranteed but, obviously for us, the producers made sure that the house met 21st-century safety regulations. Still, they also made sure the conditions were as close to reality as possible. The house had a huge courtyard, which was filled with three tonnes of mud specifically for this programme to recreate the living conditions of that time. This meant we were always dragging ourselves through the mud. For someone who likes to look presentable all the time, this wasn't something I found easy to cope with and something I could have really done without. We had no toilet inside the house, so to use it, we had to go outside, no matter whether it was nice weather or pouring down with rain late at night. Space was also limited – there were several families sleeping in the same room, so the sleeping arrangements took most people some time to get used to. Free time was very precious and a working day started very early because things just had to be done. When we did manage to have some time off, we made sure we didn't waste a single minute of it.

I'm probably painting a very gloomy picture here, but there were also happy moments. We all bonded really well and I think I made friends for life on this programme, which just goes to show that hardship brings people more closely together.

53

10 What happened before Elisa joined the show?

    A   Her friends were irritated that Elisa had not told them about the show earlier. ☐

    B   Elisa was disappointed about the lack of information she was given about the show. ☐

    C   Her mother was anxious about what the show's viewers might think of Elisa. ☐

    [1]

11 In paragraph 2, Elisa suggests that

    A   The show taught everyone a very important lesson in life. ☐

    B   Everyone on the show was very knowledgeable about history. ☐

    C   The participants preferred the simple way of life during the show. ☐

    [1]

12 How did Elisa feel about sewing clothes?

    A   She was worried it might affect her health. ☐

    B   She did not think she was given enough time to learn. ☐

    C   She found making some clothes more difficult than others. ☐

    [1]

13 What was the biggest challenge about living in a 19th-century house for Elisa?

    A   having to access certain facilities in bad weather ☐

    B   sharing her private space with other people ☐

    C   being unable to keep her clothes clean ☐

    [1]

14 What does 'gloomy' in line 53 mean?

    A   depressing ☐

    B   realistic ☐

    C   unpredictable ☐

    [1]

15 The main purpose of Elisa's blog is

    A   to describe how people's opinions about a reality show can change ☐

    B   to show people the benefits of experiencing something unusual ☐

    C   to inform people about poor living conditions in the past. ☐

                                                       [1]

                                             [Total: 6]

When you have finished doing this part of the test, go to the answer key for Section 1, Unit 1.2 and check your answers.

Your score:...................... out of 6

CHECK YOUR PROGRESS

Now think about your progress so far and answer the following questions:

- Was your score in Test 2, Exercise 4, higher than in Test 1, or not? Why do you think this is?

- After doing the **Reflection** section for this part of the exam, did you find it easier to do Test 2? What guidance did you find helpful?

- Is there anything you still find difficult? What are you going to do to improve this?

Develop your skills

In Exercise 4, you are tested on whether you can select the correct details and ideas/opinions and understand the connections between these ideas, which may be either directly stated or implied in the text. You will also be tested on understanding the text as a whole, ideas in individual paragraphs and words or phrases in some sentences.

Try the following activities to improve these reading skills:

- Read a range of online blogs, magazine articles, interviews or short stories where the author describes their experiences of something (e.g. taking up a new hobby, travelling, doing a new job, taking part in a competition, living in a new place). When you read these texts try to do different things each time.

- Read the whole text and decide why the writer wrote the text (e.g. to inform readers about a certain topic) and highlight the evidence in the text that tells you that (e.g. referring to research, statistics, providing a lot of factual information). The highlighted features should be present throughout the text. This activity will also help your writing skills.

- Quickly skim read the whole text and find the paragraphs where the writer talks about their feelings/attitudes about a process (e.g. when learning something new). Then read these paragraphs again more slowly and say how the writer's feelings/attitudes changed throughout the process.

TIP

Learning to guess unknown vocabulary from the text around it, while you are reading, will help you improve your reading speed. It is also important to have this skill as you are not allowed to use a dictionary during the exam.

- Select one paragraph and circle all the referencing words in it (e.g. *it*, *this*, *them*, *those*). Then read the sentences before and after these words and say what the words refer to. Learning more about how referencing words are used will help you improve your writing.

- Scan the whole text (or just a few paragraphs) for unknown words and phrases. Highlight this vocabulary and read a bit of text before and after it. Try to find clues in the text that will help you guess the meaning. Write down what you think the vocabulary means and then check in an English dictionary.

Writing: what are the examiners looking for?

a   The list shows features that the examiners will be looking for in your writing. Look at the list and decide whether the features are connected with content or language. Then complete the following table by listing the features under the correct heading. If you are new to the Reading and Writing exam, first look at the simplified mark scheme in the **What are the examiners looking for?** section and then do this exercise.

> **TIP**
>
> In Exercise 5, you are only tested on your writing skills. There are 6 marks available for the content of your email and 9 marks available for the language that you use.

Features

- how well you organise ideas
- how accurate the language is (i.e. grammar and vocabulary)
- how well you complete the task
- a range of vocabulary
- paragraphs
- the correct length
- the appropriate format (e.g. an email, a review)
- a range of linking words and phrases
- how well you develop ideas
- a range of grammatical structures (e.g. tenses, conditionals, relative clauses)
- the appropriate register for the intended audience (i.e. informal, formal or semi-formal)
- how relevant your ideas are
- how well you achieve the intended purpose of the task (e.g. to persuade, to inform, to evaluate)

Content (include seven points)	Language (include six points)

b   Look at the following descriptions **A–D**. They describe how well you can do things when you answer a question in the writing part of the exam. However, the descriptions are in the wrong order. Read them and place them in the correct band next to the correct marks for **content** in the following table.

A

- very few words or nothing has been written

B

- the task is fully completed
- ideas are relevant
- the format and register are appropriate throughout
- the correct purpose is achieved
- ideas are well developed
- the answer is the correct length

C

- the task is only partially completed
- some ideas are irrelevant
- the format and register are sometimes inappropriate
- the correct purpose is not achieved
- very little development of ideas
- answer may be too short

D

- the task is mainly completed
- ideas are mainly relevant
- the format and register are mostly appropriate
- the correct purpose is mostly achieved
- most ideas are developed
- the answer is the correct length

Marks	How well it is done (Content)
5–6 (top band)	
3–4 (middle band)	
1–2 (low band)	
0	

c   Now do the same with the descriptions of how well you use the language in your own writing in the following table.

TIP

When you have completed the tables in Exercises b and c, use them as simplified mark schemes to mark your own writing. Before you decide on the marks for content and language, think about the band first: top band (excellent skills), middle band (reasonable skills) and low band (poor skills). Then decide on the exact mark; the higher the mark, the more things you do well in that band.

A

- a range of common words, only a few less common words
- a range of simple grammatical structures, only a few complex structures
- mostly accurate
- most errors appear in less common words and more complex structures
- the meaning is always clear despite all the errors
- ideas are reasonably well organised into paragraphs
- a range of linking words and phrases

B

- a very good range of common and less common words
- a very good range of simple and complex grammatical structures
- very few errors
- errors only appear in less common words and complex grammatical structures
- the meaning is always clear despite errors
- ideas are well organised into paragraphs
- a very good range of linking words and phrases

C

- very few words or nothing has been written

D

- a small range of only common words
- a small range of only simple grammatical structures
- frequent errors
- errors appear in common words and simple grammatical structures
- the meaning is sometimes unclear because of errors
- very little attempt at organising ideas into paragraphs
- a small range of only simple linking words

Marks	How well it is done (Language)
7–9 (top band)	
4–6 (middle band)	
1–3 (low band)	
0	

First, do the following writing exercise as you would in the real exam. Then look at the **Reflection** section to see some guidance on how to do this type of exercise. Also, look at the **Learn from mistakes** section to see common mistakes made by other students. Finally, do the same type of exercise in Test 2 to see if you have improved.

Test 1

Exercise 5

16 Your family has recently got a new pet.

Write an email to a friend about the pet.

In your email, you should:

- describe your new pet

- explain what you do to look after your new pet

- say how the pet makes you feel and why.

Write about 120 to 160 words.

You will receive up to 6 marks for the content of your email, and up to 9 marks for the language used.

[Total: 15]

When you have finished doing this part of the test, go to the answer key for Section 1, Unit 1.2. Read the model answer and compare the content and language used in this email with your email. Then look at the simplified mark scheme for Exercise 5 in the **What are the examiners looking for?** section. Try to guess what marks you might get for the content and language in your email.

Your score for content: .... out of 6

Your score for language: .... out of 9

Reflection

Now think about the way you did Test 1, Exercise 5. Read the questions in the following table and put YES or NO to show you have, or have not, done these things. The questions remind you about the things you should do in Exercise 5 in the Reading and Writing exam. If some of your answers are NO, these are the areas you need to practise a bit more to improve your performance in the exam.

Before you started writing	YES or NO	Guidance
1 Did you read the instructions carefully and highlight the important information?		Pay attention to the information in the instructions, which tell you what you have to do: • what format you should write in (e.g. an email) • who you are writing to (e.g. a friend) • what points you need to include (e.g. describe your new pet). Remember – you need to cover all three points in your email • how many words you should write.
2 Did you plan your answer before you started writing?		Spend a few moments thinking about how you are going to organise your email, how many paragraphs to include and what ideas you want to include in each paragraph. Only make quick notes of these ideas (e.g. *cat / rescue home, brown, feed and play / happy, mischievous*). Do not spend too much time writing down your notes as long sentences.
3 Did you decide what register your email should be in?		Always check who you are writing to before deciding what register you need. If you are writing to a friend, you need to write in an informal register.
While you were writing	YES or NO	Guidance
4 Did you refer to your notes from the planning stage?		Your notes will save you time when you start writing your answer. You will already know what information you need to include and in which order. Also, as you will already know what to write, it is easier for you to focus on other things in your writing, like grammar and vocabulary.
5 Did you develop the ideas from the bullet points?		Do not just include short answers to the bullet points. Develop your ideas by adding examples, comparing things that are happening now with something in the past, or comparing your situation with somebody else's (e.g. another family member, your neighbour).
6 Did you make sure you divided your email into paragraphs?		Start with three paragraphs (1 introduction, 2 giving information, 3 conclusion). If you write about more topics, you can add more paragraphs in the middle.
7 Did you make sure you used linking words and phrases to connect ideas?		Connect your ideas in sentences within paragraphs (e.g. *when, but, that is why, which*). You also need linkers to introduce a new idea at the start of a paragraph (e.g. *anyway, that reminds me*). Without any linkers your writing will sound very simple and unnatural.

While you were writing	YES or NO	Guidance
8 Did you use a range of vocabulary?		To increase your range of vocabulary try using: • synonyms (e.g. *huge, enormous, massive, look, stare, glance*) • collocations (e.g. *keep a promise, the exact opposite*) • phrasal verbs (e.g. *break up for the summer, grow up in town*) • idioms (e.g. *she is a breath of fresh air, he makes my day*) • other fixed expressions (e.g. *I am in charge of, we are out of time*).
9 Did you use a range of grammatical structures?		Use a range of structures – such as tenses (e.g. *I was so happy because my parents had got me a pet*), or conditionals (e.g. *If I had not asked every single day, my parents would not have agreed to get me a pet*).
After you finished writing	**YES or NO**	**Guidance**
10 Did you check that you covered all three points from the question and achieved the purpose of the task (e.g. to inform and explain)?		You might lose marks for content if you do not cover all three points from the question.
11 Did you check that your email is within the word limit?		If you write too little, your answer will not be developed enough and you might lose marks for content. If you spend too much time on your answer and it is too long, some of your ideas may be irrelevant to the task and you might not have enough time for the other parts of the test.
12 Did you proofread your answer to check for any obvious errors?		When you proofread your writing, check if your verbs are in the correct form (e.g. *see/sees/saw/seen/seeing*), you used the correct prepositions (e.g. *in/at/with/by*), you used articles (*a/the*), you used the correct tenses (e.g. *he went / he was going / he will go / he is gone*) and so on. However, only do this if you have enough time. Remember that you still have to write another task after Exercise 5.

If you answered 'No' to any of the questions in the **Reflection** section, try to follow all the guidance from this section when you do Test 2, Exercise 5.

Learn from mistakes

a   Before you do Test 2, Exercise 5, look at two emails written by students A and B. Read the emails and decide which one is better, and why.

b   Then look at the simplified mark scheme for Exercise 5 in the **What are the examiners looking for?** section. How many marks do you think each student would receive for the content and language? Then check your suggestions for the marks in the answer key for Section 1, Unit 1.2.

Student A's email

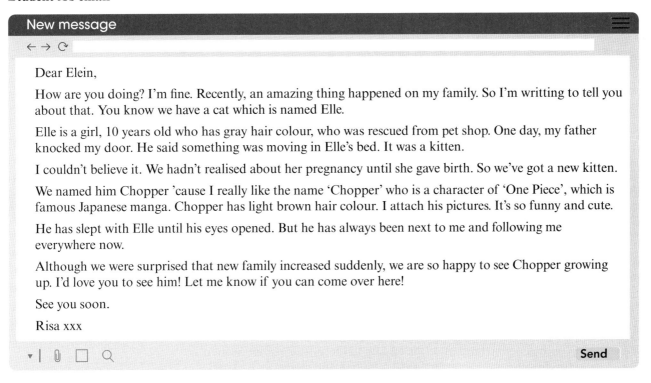

New message

← → ↻

Dear Elein,

How are you doing? I'm fine. Recently, an amazing thing happened on my family. So I'm writting to tell you about that. You know we have a cat which is named Elle.

Elle is a girl, 10 years old who has gray hair colour, who was rescued from pet shop. One day, my father knocked my door. He said something was moving in Elle's bed. It was a kitten.

I couldn't believe it. We hadn't realised about her pregnancy until she gave birth. So we've got a new kitten.

We named him Chopper 'cause I really like the name 'Chopper' who is a character of 'One Piece', which is famous Japanese manga. Chopper has light brown hair colour. I attach his pictures. It's so funny and cute.

He has slept with Elle until his eyes opened. But he has always been next to me and following me everywhere now.

Although we were surprised that new family increased suddenly, we are so happy to see Chopper growing up. I'd love you to see him! Let me know if you can come over here!

See you soon.

Risa xxx

▾ | 🖉 ▢ 🔍   Send

Student B's email

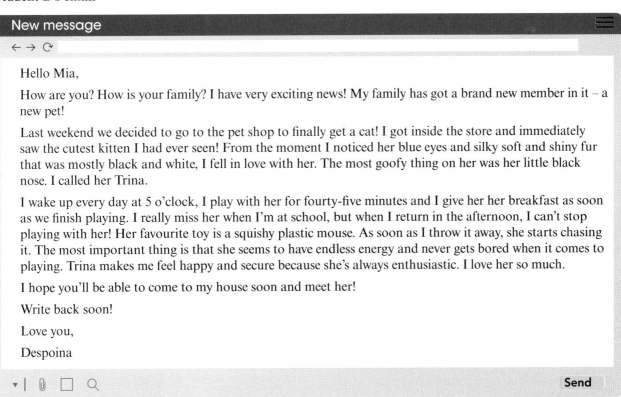

New message

← → ↻

Hello Mia,

How are you? How is your family? I have very exciting news! My family has got a brand new member in it – a new pet!

Last weekend we decided to go to the pet shop to finally get a cat! I got inside the store and immediately saw the cutest kitten I had ever seen! From the moment I noticed her blue eyes and silky soft and shiny fur that was mostly black and white, I fell in love with her. The most goofy thing on her was her little black nose. I called her Trina.

I wake up every day at 5 o'clock, I play with her for fourty-five minutes and I give her her breakfast as soon as we finish playing. I really miss her when I'm at school, but when I return in the afternoon, I can't stop playing with her! Her favourite toy is a squishy plastic mouse. As soon as I throw it away, she starts chasing it. The most important thing is that she seems to have endless energy and never gets bored when it comes to playing. Trina makes me feel happy and secure because she's always enthusiastic. I love her so much.

I hope you'll be able to come to my house soon and meet her!

Write back soon!

Love you,

Despoina

▾ | 🖉 ▢ 🔍   Send

Now do Test 2, Exercise 5, and remember to follow all the guidance from the **Reflection** section for Test 1.

Test 2

Exercise 5

16 You have just finished working on a school project.

Write an email to a friend about the project.

In your email, you should:

- say what the project was about
- say how successful the project was, and why
- explain what you would have done differently.

Write about 120 to 160 words.

You will receive up to 6 marks for the content of your email, and up to 9 marks for the language used.

[Total: 15]

When you have finished doing this part of the test, go to the answer key for Section 1, Unit 1.2. Read the model answer and compare the content and language used in this email with your email. Then look at the simplified mark scheme for Exercise 5 in the **What are the examiners looking for?** section. Try to guess what marks you might get for the content and language in your email.

Your score for content:................... out of 6

Your score for language:................... out of 9

CHECK YOUR PROGRESS

Now think about your progress so far and answer the following questions:

- Was your score in Test 2, Exercise 5, higher than in Test 1, or not? Why do you think this is?
- After doing the **Reflection** section for this part of the exam, did you find it easier to do Test 2? What guidance did you find helpful?
- Is there anything you still find difficult? What are you going to do to improve this?

Develop your skills

In Exercise 5, you are tested on your writing skills. These include:

- communicating your ideas clearly
- organising and linking your ideas logically

- using a range of grammatical structures and vocabulary accurately

- using the appropriate format and register.

Try the following activities to improve your writing skills.

- Write in English as much as you can (e.g. your school notes, memos, emails to friends, text messages, keep a diary).

- Find a text online. Cut and paste into a document and remove all the paragraphs so that the text is not divided into sections at all. Then read the text and try to divide it into logical paragraphs.

- Find a short text online and cut and paste one paragraph into a document. Then blank out all the linking words (e.g. *but*, *when*, *which*, *however*). Read the text and insert the linking words back into the text. Compare your rewritten text with the original one to check your answers.

- Keep a notebook with your own common mistakes and write the corrections next to the mistakes.

- When you look up a new word/phrase in an English dictionary, also copy the sentence that shows you how to use the word/phrase, do not just copy the definition/meaning. This will make it easier for you to use the word correctly in your speaking and writing. It will also help you improve your sentence structures.

Test 1

Exercise 6

17 Your class recently went on a trip to your capital city. Your teacher has now asked you to write a report about the trip.

In your report, say what you enjoyed about the trip and suggest how school trips can be improved in the future.

Here are some comments from other students:

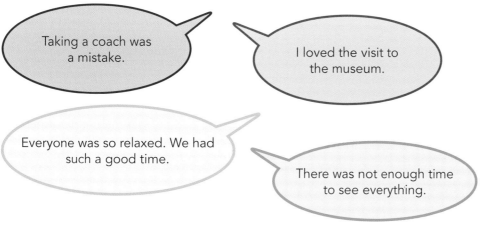

Taking a coach was a mistake.

I loved the visit to the museum.

Everyone was so relaxed. We had such a good time.

There was not enough time to see everything.

> **TIP**
>
> The prompts in Exercise 6 give you ideas for your writing. However, if you prefer, you can use only your own ideas. If you choose to use the ideas from the prompts you should paraphrase them, develop them and also add ideas of your own.

Now write a report for your teacher.

The comments above may give you some ideas, and you should also use some ideas of your own.

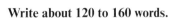

Write about 120 to 160 words.

You will receive up to 6 marks for the content of your report, and up to 9 marks for the language used.

[Total: 15]

When you have finished doing this part of the test, go to the answer key for Section 1, Unit 1.2. Read the model answer and compare the content and language used in this report with your report. Then look at the simplified mark scheme for Exercise 6 in the **What are the examiners looking for?** section. Try to guess what mark you might get for the content and language in your report.

> Your score for content:...................... out of 6
>
> Your score for language:...................... out of 9

Reflection

Now think about the way you did Test 1, Exercise 6. Read the questions in the following table and put YES or NO to show you have, or have not, done these things. The questions remind you about the things you should do in Exercise 6 in the Writing exam. If some of your answers are NO, these are the areas you need to practise a bit more to improve your performance in the Writing exam.

Before you started writing	YES or NO	Guidance
1 Did you read the instructions carefully and highlight the important information?		Pay attention to the information in the instructions, which tell you what you have to do: • what format you should write (e.g. a report) • who you are writing to (e.g. a teacher) • what you need to include (e.g. what you enjoyed and suggest improvements) • how many words you should write (120–160).
2 Did you plan your answer before you started writing?		Spend a few moments thinking about: • what the purpose of the report is • what register you should use (i.e. informal, semi-formal or formal) • how many paragraphs to include • what ideas you want to include in each paragraph. Only make quick notes of these ideas (e.g. *coach – bad traffic, delays / ran out of time to see more / museum – good, but guided tour would be better / recommendations – students vote on what to see, more careful planning next time, by train*).

While you were writing	YES or NO	Guidance
3 Did you refer to your notes from the planning stage?		It is very difficult to think of ideas and write at the same time. If you have your notes from the planning stage, you know you will not forget to mention anything and your ideas will be well organised, in a logical order.
4 Did you paraphrase the ideas from the speech bubbles (if you used them)?		
5 Did you also include at least one idea of your own?		
6 Did you develop your ideas?		Develop your ideas by adding examples, or writing about the positive and also negative aspects (e.g. what was good about the museum and what was not). You can also include reasons and explanations.
7 Did you divide your report into paragraphs?		You should always have at least three paragraphs. If you have a lot of information in the middle paragraph, you can divide it into more paragraphs (e.g. the positive and negative points about the trip).
8 Did you label paragraphs / report sections with subheadings?		To make it easier for the reader to find the necessary information in reports, we use subheadings for paragraphs (e.g. *1 Introduction, 2 The trip, 3 Conclusion / Recommendations*).
9 Did you introduce the topic of the report in the first paragraph?		To introduce your report, use phrases like *The aim of this report is to …* or *This report provides information about …* .
10 Did you provide information about the trip in the middle paragraph?		
11 Did you suggest improvements in the last paragraph?		To make recommendations in the final paragraph of your report, use phrases like *I therefore suggest (+ -ing form)* or *I would like to recommend that …* .
12 Did you use linking words and phrases to connect ideas?		In reports we often use linking words and phrases to add more examples (e.g. *in addition to that*), contrast (e.g. *however*) and result (e.g. *therefore*).
13 Did you make sure your report is written in the correct register?		The register is the tone and the type of language you use in your writing. The register needs to be appropriate for the given situation. Always check who you are writing to before deciding on the register. If you are writing to your teacher, you need to use a semi-formal register.

While you were writing	YES or NO	Guidance
14 Did you try to use a range of grammatical structures?		• Use a range of structures, like tenses (e.g. *We had been driving on the motorway for an hour when we experienced bad traffic and we were delayed as a result*), or conditionals (e.g. *If we had not taken a coach, we would have had more time to see the city centre properly*). • It is common to use the passive voice in reports. This makes them a bit more formal. For example, rather than writing 'they were renovating one section of the museum', you can write 'one section of the museum was being renovated'.
15 Did you use a range of words and phrases?		In reports you will often be asked to provide opinions and to evaluate something. This means you can use a range of adjectives. Remember that your choice of vocabulary needs to be appropriate for a semi-formal register so, instead of using *It was rubbish*, you should write *It was very disappointing* or *It did not meet our expectations*.
After you finished writing	YES or NO	Guidance
16 Did you check that your report is within the word limit?		
17 Did you proofread your report at the end?		Only check your writing if you have some time left and you have completed all the other parts of the Reading and Writing exam.

If you answered 'No' to any of the questions in the **Reflection** section, try to follow all the guidance from this section when you do Test 2, Exercise 6.

Learn from mistakes

a   Before you do Test 2, Exercise 6, look at two reports written by students A and B. Read the reports and decide which one is better, and why.

b   Then look at the simplified mark scheme for Exercise 6 in the **What are the examiners looking for?** section. How many marks do you think each student would receive for the content and language? Then check your suggestions for the marks in the answer key for Section 1, Unit 1.2.

Student A's report

Introduction

The principal aims of this report are to describe how the school trip was and explain how people enjoyed as well as things they did not like.

Student's opinions about the first moments

Having made a survey with 30 students we could see many different opinions about the trip. No sooner had we arrived to the first city that a group of students were complaining about the coach. The fact that this did not have toilet, for a long trip, was a big issue. However, some students saw here a possibility to stop frecuently and chat with other student different than the ones around them.

The visit

Most of them, nearly three quarters, enjoyed the trip in general. The best part was the museum, however some of them did not have enough time to visit everything because some roads were closed. In addition, we missed the main square of the city.

Recommendations

In light of the results above, I recommend the following:

• to check every road before leaving in order to know the route we should follow.
• to rent a coach with toilet and stop less frecuently using this time to visit the city.

Following these recommendations, next trips will be improved as well as the number of participants.

Student B's report

This report is about my class recently went on a trip to Seoul. Seoul is South Korea's capital. We planned to visit three tourist attractions.

First, we visited Gyeongbokgung Palace. This traditional palace is located in centre of Seoul. The palace was really beautiful and exotic. I enjoyed the palace view. Also, we went to the National Palace museum. I love the visit to the museum.
Second place is Insa-dong. The Insa-dong is traditional culture area. The Insa-dong was closed to the palace. We moved to the Insa-dong by walk. There were many restaurants, shops, street shops. We ate Korean traditional foods, Bulgogi and Bibimhap. It was really tasty. Some students bought a Korean traditional souvenir here. We wanted to stay longer, but there wasn't enough time to see everything.

Finally, we moved to Han-river Park. We took a coach to go there. However, we spent much time on the roads. There was a lot of traffic. Taking a coach was a mistake. After arrived the Han-river Park, we rode a bycles. It was really exciting. What is more, view of the Han-river Park is very nice. Also, we laid picnic mat on the grass. Everyone was so relaxed. We had a good time.

Test 2

Exercise 6

17 In your lesson you were talking about libraries. Your teacher has asked you to write a report about your school library.

In your report you should say what you like about the school library and suggest how it can be improved.

Here are some comments from other students:

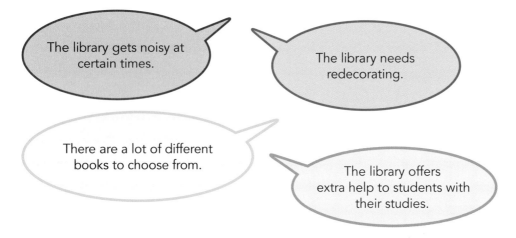

The library gets noisy at certain times.

The library needs redecorating.

There are a lot of different books to choose from.

The library offers extra help to students with their studies.

Now write a report for your teacher.

The comments above may give you some ideas, and you should also use some ideas of your own.

Write about 120 to 160 words.

You will receive up to 6 marks for the content of your report, and up to 9 marks for the language used.

[Total: 15]

When you have finished doing this part of the test, go to the answer key for Section 1, Unit 1.2. Read the model answer and compare the content and language used in this report with your report. Then look at the simplified mark scheme for Exercise 6 in the **What are the examiners looking for?** section. Try to guess what mark you might get for the content and language in your report.

> Your score for content:................... out of 6
>
> Your score for language:................... out of 9

Now think about your progress so far and answer the following questions:

- Was your score in Test 2, Exercise 6, higher than in Test 1, or not? Why do you think this is?

- After doing the **Reflection** section for this part of the exam, did you find it easier to do Test 2? What guidance did you find helpful?

- Is there anything you still find difficult? What are you going to do to improve this?

Develop your skills

In Exercise 6, you are tested on the same writing skills as in Exercise 5. These include:

- communicating your ideas clearly

- organising and linking your ideas logically

- using a range of grammatical structures and vocabulary accurately

- using the appropriate format and register.

Try the following activity to practise writing in different formats and using the appropriate register:

- Find examples of different types of texts online (e.g. cover letters, essays, reports, customer reviews, blogs, complaint letters). Read them and think who the intended audience is (e.g. the wider public, teenagers, someone in charge) and what the purpose of the text is (e.g. to complain, to entertain, to educate). Notice the language each text uses and how different the language is from another type of text. Also think whether the language sounds more formal (e.g. a cover letter, report), semi-formal (customer reviews) or informal (blogs, posts on social media). Then try to rewrite these texts using a different style and register. For example, rewriting a formal report as an informal email to a friend.

Also try the activities from the **Develop your skills** section for Exercise 5 to improve the rest of your writing skills.

> **TIP**
>
> Remember – you learn most from your own mistakes. To improve your writing in general, always rewrite your first drafts after they have been corrected by your teacher.

Unit 1.3: Language focus

First, do the exercise in Test 3 as you would in the real exam. Then, before you check your answers, look at the **Language focus** section and follow the instructions.

Test 3

Exercise 1

Read the article about the two largest caves in the world, located in Asia, and then answer the questions.

The largest caves in the world

Son Doong Cave in Vietnam

Son Doong Cave, situated in a national park in central Vietnam, was discovered by a local man called Ho Khanh in the early 1990s. Ho liked to trek through the park. One day he thought he could hear a river from inside a hill, which, on its own, isn't unusual. When he came closer, however, he could feel wind blowing from an opening in a cliff. This suggested that the opening wasn't just a small hole, but something much bigger. After returning to the village, he forgot all about his discovery. It wasn't until 2008 when Ho came across the same opening again. This time, he took careful notes of the location and passed them on to the caving professionals, who carried out their initial research of the cave in 2009. They looked at the structure of the cave, but the cave was so large they couldn't finish mapping it until 2010, when they became aware that Doong was, indeed, the largest cave ever found. In fact, the cave is so huge, with a length of 5 kilometres and a height of 200 metres, that several skyscrapers could easily fit inside it.

After studying the rocks, scientists were able to determine the cave's age. While other cave systems in the area of the national park are as old as 450 million years, Son Doong is relatively young and goes back only 3 million years. New hollow spaces inside the cave were created by a river about 300,000 years ago. In some parts of the cave the ceiling of these hollow spaces

collapsed, which allowed the direct sunlight in. It was just a matter of time before plants and animals made it their home and the cave now contains its own jungle. The unique ecosystem that has been created has been carefully examined by scientists as it may reveal exciting new discoveries. And that is also one of the reasons why access to Son Doong is restricted to a certain number of visitors each year.

Deer Cave in Malaysia

Deer Cave, the second largest cave in the world, was first explored in 1961. Scientists have since documented the various living organisms that have made the place their home. The name for the cave didn't come from its appearance or a special feature inside it. It's believed that deer came to lick salt off the rocks at the cave's entrance.

The cave is a popular tourist attraction, bringing annual crowds of over 25,000 visitors to the area. Tourists are especially drawn to the 30 species of bats that can be found there. To reach the cave, visitors take a three-kilometre walk through the surrounding jungle, which is home to various species of monkeys and birds.

1   How did the local man know there was a cave?

.... [1]

2   When did experts explore Son Doong Cave for the first time?

.... [1]

3   How old is Son Doong Cave?

.... [1]

4   How did Deer Cave get its name?

.... [1]

5   What is Deer Cave most famous for?

.... [1]

6   What did the caving experts research inside the two caves? Give **three** details.

....

....

.... [3]

[Total: 8]

TIP

Remember, apart from the correct detail for each question in this exercise, there is sometimes distracting information in the text. This information is to test your reading skills for detail to see whether you can select the correct answer.

Language focus

After you have answered all the questions in Exercise 1, look at the **Language focus** box following each question. These boxes contain guidance that will help you focus on the important vocabulary and grammar that you need to select the correct answer. Then read the text again to check if you selected the correct answers the first time.

1   How did the local man know there was a cave?

.... [1]

LANGUAGE FOCUS 1

There are two situations mentioned. One is the correct answer and one is a distracting detail. Which situation made Ho think there might be a cave? Which phrase tells you that?

2 When did experts explore Son Doong Cave for the first time?

.... [1]

LANGUAGE FOCUS 2

There are several years mentioned in the text. However, in which year did experts start exploring the cave?

'Experts' is paraphrased in the text. What word is used instead?

Which phrase in the text means 'explore for the first time'?

---

3 How old is Son Doong Cave?

.... [1]

LANGUAGE FOCUS 3

There are three details referring to how old something is. What do these details refer to? Which one refers only to Son Doong Cave?

---

4 How did Deer Cave get its name?

.... [1]

LANGUAGE FOCUS 4

Find the reference to the 'name'. There are three details, but only one is correct. Which phrase tells you which two are wrong?

---

5 What is Deer Cave most famous for?

.... [1]

LANGUAGE FOCUS 5

The phrase 'most famous' in the question is important. How is it paraphrased in the text? The answer comes straight after this phrase.

---

6   What did the caving experts research inside the two caves? Give **three** details.

....

....

.... [3]

LANGUAGE FOCUS 6

Think of synonyms (i.e. similar words) for 'to research something' and 'experts'. These synonyms will help you to find some of the answers in the text.

When you have finished doing this part of the test and the **Language focus** section, go to the answer key for Section 1, Unit 1.3 and check your answers.

Your score:...................... out of 8

CHECK YOUR PROGRESS

Now think about your progress so far and answer the following questions:

*   Did you remember to use all the exam techniques you learnt in Unit 1.2, Exercise 1?

*   Was your score in Exercise 1 in this unit better or worse than your scores in Exercise 1 in Unit 1.2? Why do you think this is?

*   After looking at the **Language focus** sections for this part of the exam, did you find it easier to find the correct answers? Are you now better at recognising what the correct detail is and what the distracting information is?

*   Is there anything that you still find difficult? What are you going to do to improve this?

Test 3

Exercise 2

Read the magazine article about four people (**A–D**) and what they say about sports facilities and exercising. Then answer Question **7**.

TIP

The number of texts in Exercise 2 may vary from one long text to five shorter ones.

Do you like to exercise regularly?

A: Abhay

In the past, I would only go skiing in the mountains or play beach volleyball once or twice a year during my holidays. My wife and kids tried to persuade me to go to the local sports centre more often, but I'd always come up with an excuse. This was all before I was involved in a skiing accident one winter and needed physiotherapy. My doctor also suggested going to the gym, so I did. My family have noticed that I don't get so stressed out anymore and I think they're right. At work, I don't really have time to socialise, but at the gym it's a different story. There's always someone who invites the others for a coffee and I love getting to know them. My wife can't understand why I resisted going to the gym for so long. I definitely want to keep it up and disagree with anybody who says that our local sports centre is not worth the money.

B: Bibi

I really take pride in staying in shape. To achieve this, I'm very particular about what I eat, but also about my fitness regime. I try to keep active as often as I can, even though it's a real challenge to motivate myself sometimes, especially when I get home tired after work. I wish I had a personal trainer to push me, but I find monthly gym fees really high. Some of my work colleagues go to the gym and say it's a good place to switch off after work and meet someone else, rather than the people you spend all day with. However, I think I've found a good alternative, which I've grown to like much more than going to the gym. I go jogging in my local park four times a week. My friend thinks that I overdo the jogging. She also worries it's too dangerous and I might fall over and hurt my ankle. But then that can happen anywhere.

C: Conor

These days, I think it's very important to make sure everyone gets enough exercise because most people have jobs where they don't move enough all day long. However, I feel everything should be done in moderation, unlike quite a few of my colleagues who are obsessed with extreme workouts. I've recently started cycling to work. I also go swimming twice a week with my friend. I think swimming is great and quite effective as part of injury recovery, just like in the case of my friend. He felt a bit anxious about going on his own, so asked me to come along. I thought it'd be good for me to get a bit more active because I noticed that I got quite breathless and had put on a bit of weight. As a result of our swimming practice, my friend made a full recovery and I improved my stamina, which made me think I should have taken up swimming ages ago.

D: Dana

I enjoy sports and take looking after my health very seriously. I read lots of articles related to exercising and how it impacts how people feel. I do lots of outdoor activities from playing tennis to trekking and, when the weather gets bad, I do indoor activities like squash or Zumba. However, it took me a while to find a sports centre close to my house. I think this is one of the things that puts people off joining sports centres. Some say the cost is an important factor too. I pay quite a lot for my annual membership, but I expect the best in return, which, sadly, hasn't been the case this year. A few weeks ago, I visited a friend and she took me to her local sports centre. I couldn't believe the range of activities they offered to attract all ages. I do believe it's important to start with sports as early in life as possible.

For each question, write the correct letter A, B, C or D on the line.

7   Which person…

    a   says they started working out after an injury? .... [1]

    b   regrets not starting exercising earlier in life? .... [1]

    c   claims it is more difficult to exercise on their own? .... [1]

    d   suggests there are not enough local sports facilities? .... [1]

e	thinks a lot of people exercise too much these days? .... [1]
f	feels exercising positively affects their mood? .... [1]
g	prefers to do their exercises outdoors? .... [1]
h	is disappointed with the service at their sports centre? .... [1]
i	thinks going to the gym is a good way of meeting people? .... [1]

[Total: 9]

TIP

In Exercise 2, most of the ideas/opinions from the list in the question will only be implied in the texts. This means the ideas/opinions will not be directly stated. This can be done in many different ways. For example: by providing examples of the idea/opinion or suggesting a possible result of a situation (*if you climb that tree, you might fall* implies it is dangerous to climb trees).

Language focus

Before you check your answers for Test 3 Exercise 2, do this **Language focus** section. It will help you to decide whether you have selected the correct opinions as your answers.

a In addition to the correct answers, each text also contains distracting ideas/opinions. Look at the opinions listed. Some of them are the correct answers and some of them are the distracting details. Read the four texts again and decide which opinions are the distractors and why they are the wrong answers.

TIP

Before you make your final choice, make sure that the whole idea in the opinion is expressed in the text. If only one word, or part of the opinion, is expressed in the text this means it is probably one of the distractors and not the correct answer.

A: Abhay

a says they started working out after an injury?
b regrets not starting exercising earlier in life?
f feels exercising positively affects their mood?
g prefers to do their exercises outdoors?
i thinks going to the gym is a good way of meeting people?

B: Bibi

a says they started working out after an injury?
c claims it is more difficult to exercise on their own?
e thinks a lot of people exercise too much these days?
g prefers to do their exercises outdoors?
i thinks going to the gym is a good way of meeting people?

C: Conor

a says they started working out after an injury?
b regrets not starting exercising earlier in life?
c claims it is more difficult to exercise on their own?
e thinks a lot of people exercise too much these days?
f feels exercising positively affects their mood?

D: Dana

b regrets not starting exercising earlier in life?
c claims it is more difficult to exercise on their own?
d suggests there are not enough local sports facilities?
f feels exercising positively affects their mood?
g prefers to do their exercises outdoors?
h is disappointed with the service at their sports centre?

b Now you are going to focus on the vocabulary used in the opinions (a)–(i) and the four texts in Exercise 2. Read the texts again and find the words and phrases that express a very similar idea to the vocabulary listed. This vocabulary will help you with matching the ideas/opinions (a)–(i) to the correct texts **A–D**.

A Abhay

a   an injury – ....

b   I started working out – ....

c   positively affects their mood – ....

d   I feel that – ....

e   meeting people – ....

f   there – ....

g   it is a good way of – ....

B Bibi

a   it is more difficult – ....

b   on their own – ....

c   prefers – ....

d   outdoors – ....

e   sports facilities – ....

f   too expensive – ....

C Conor

a   regrets not starting – ....

b   exercising – ....

c   earlier in life – ....

d   a lot of people – ....

e   exercise – ....

f   too much – ....

D Dana

a   there are not enough – ....

b   sports facilities – ....

c   local – ....

d   is disappointed with – ....

e   the service – ....

When you have finished doing this part of the test and the Language focus section, go to the answer key for Section 1, Unit 1.3 and check your answers.

Your score:..................... out of 9

TIP

The vocabulary in the **Language focus** sections is useful for your own speaking and writing. For example, use the vocabulary from this section to talk about your own experience of keeping fit and using sports facilities.

CHECK YOUR PROGRESS

Now think about your progress so far and answer the following questions:

- Did you remember to use all the exam techniques you learnt in Unit 1.2, Exercise 2?

- Was your score in Exercise 2 in this unit better or worse than your scores in Exercise 2 in Unit 1.2? Why do you think this is?

- After looking at the **Language focus** sections for this part of the exam, did you find it easier to find the correct answers? Are you now better at recognising what the correct opinion is and what the distracting information is?

- What do you still find difficult? What are you going to do to improve this?

Test 3

Exercise 3

Read the following blog, written by Harrison Green, about his trek along the edge of the Himalayas, and then complete the notes.

Trekking in the Himalayas

This is the beginning of my journey along the edge of the highest mountain range in the world – the Himalayas.

Afghanistan and Pakistan

I started my trek with two close friends, Arzad and Sadiq. It's important to have someone with you in case of emergency, but also to keep you company during a long journey. Plus, we relied on Arzad to interpret for us to make sure that communicating with the locals, which could have been an issue, wasn't.

We began in the Wakhan Corridor in north-east Afghanistan. The mountainous landscape makes it extremely difficult to live in for the people who've made this valley their home. We walked for miles before coming across a nomadic tribe – the Whaki people. I found them fascinating and I'd love to put a book together with all the information I collected about this tribe. We spent a day with them and told them about our plans to cross over the mountains to Pakistan. Using their local knowledge, they warned us there was still too much snow and ice in the mountains. However, we decided to set out the following morning anyway. After a few hours, I realised the nomads were right. The thin air at this high altitude also made it almost impossible for me to breathe. I was so relieved when we finally made it to Pakistan, but I definitely want to come back to this part of the world again.

India and Nepal

One day, while crossing the mountains from Pakistan to India, we got lost just before dusk. This is not a good situation to find yourself in when you only have about an hour of daylight left. The possibility of an encounter with a roaming bear or wolf was making me quite nervous. Fortunately, we managed to find a hut built by nomadic goat herders – and that's where we spent the night. The following morning, we descended to a nearby village, where we topped up our food supplies. The villagers advised us not to carry on with our journey down the tarmac road because of charging elephants. However, we took our chances and continued as planned. We didn't meet any elephants that day.

The danger came much later when we were in the Bardia National Park in Nepal. We set up our camp, close to a river. I was totally unaware of the heavy rain pouring down that night, until I heard my friends shout: 'Get out of the tent, quick!' The floodwater from the river was getting dangerously close to the tent.

In the morning, the sun came out again and everything that had happened the night before seemed like a distant memory. As we were leaving the National Park, I couldn't stop thinking about how beautiful and varied the habitats are in this region. I decided that I really needed to raise awareness of all the endangered species living here, once I got back home.

Our final destination – Bhutan – was still several hundred miles away.

Imagine you are going to give a talk about Harrison Green's Himalayan trek to your classmates. Use words from his blog to help you write some notes.

Make short notes under each heading.

8   Difficulties Harrison experienced on his trek

- ....

- ....

- ....

- ....

- ....   [5]

9 What Harrison is planning to do in the future

- ....

- .... [2]

[Total: 7]

Language focus

After you have answered the questions in Exercise 3, look at the **Language focus** box following each question. These boxes contain guidance that will help you focus on the important vocabulary and grammar that you need to select the correct answer. Then read the text again to check if you selected the correct answers the first time.

8 Difficulties Harrison experienced on his trek

- ....

- ....

- ....

- ....

- .... [5]

> TIP

To find the necessary details in the text more easily, look for certain 'clues' in the text. These are words and phrases that will lead you towards the part of the text where the detail is located. They can come before the answer but also after the answer.

LANGUAGE FOCUS 8

a What are the words/phrases in the text that introduce the idea of difficulties and dangerous situations?

b Now look at the difficulties and dangerous situations you have found in the text. Some of them are the correct answers, but some of them are distractors. To decide which ideas are the correct answers, think about which situations:

i   happened to Harrison

ii were a possibility, but didn't really happen to Harrison

iii are linked to other people.

---

9 What Harrison is planning to do in the future

- ....

- .... [2]

LANGUAGE FOCUS 9

The heading asks you to look for future plans/intentions. Which phrases tell you what Harrison would like to do?

When you have finished doing this part of the test and the **Language focus** section, go to the answer key for Section 1, Unit 1.3 and check your answers.

Your score:...................... out of 7

CHECK YOUR PROGRESS

Now think about your progress so far and answer the following questions:

- Did you remember to use all the exam techniques you learnt in Unit 1.2, Exercise 3?

- Was your score in Exercise 3 in this unit better or worse than your scores for Exercise 3 in Unit 1.2? Why do you think this is?

- After looking at the **Language focus** sections for this part of the exam, was it easier to find the correct answers?

- Is there anything that you still find difficult? What are you going to do to improve this?

Test 3

Exercise 4

Read the blog written by someone who loves foreign languages, and then answer the questions.

How many languages can you speak?

Ever since I can remember I've been fascinated by languages. The first foreign language I learnt at school was Russian. I was nine and couldn't wait to start. I adored my teacher and she made the lessons very exciting. After one year, I could read and write in a foreign language! I was very young, so didn't get anxious when it came to things like pronunciation, unlike some grown-ups. With time, I became more and more confident and could even read short stories in Russian. This was before the internet, so I couldn't just go online to practise listening. You can imagine my joy when I got a record with Russian songs for my birthday, by a singer called Alla Pugacheva. I couldn't get enough of it. I struggled to understand what Alla was singing about, but wouldn't stop playing it until I did.

I didn't start learning English until I was 14. I can't say I enjoyed my English lessons as much as I did my Russian ones. It felt like all we did were grammar exercises and never got onto speaking the language. Everything changed when my grandad told me about the time he went to live in London when he was

about my age – so, when I turned 18, I applied to study English in the United Kingdom. My parents were worried about me, in their eyes I was still a little girl. They never thought I could make it by myself, let alone in another country!

I got into a school in Manchester and couldn't wait to learn the language in the country where it's spoken. At first, the local accent made English sound a bit alien to me, but after a few weeks I noticed I could understand more and

36 | more and began to enjoy myself. I also made new friends from all over the world and being able to communicate with them in English was a dream come true. When my best friend asked me to come to Switzerland with her for a holiday, I jumped at the chance. I loved the country so much that I decided to stay longer to learn Italian, French and German – the languages spoken in Switzerland. It was the start of a very exciting journey.

Switzerland is one of many countries where there's more than one official language. I must admit – I was a bit jealous of my new friends who grew up being bilingual or, in some cases, even multilingual. I thought how wonderful it must be to speak two or more languages at home because your parents come from two different parts of the world. I became so fascinated I did quite a lot of research into

being bilingual. One American survey, done a few years ago, revealed that one in five children over the age of five speak another language at home on top of English. Another study, carried out in a nursery school, has revealed that bilingual children can come up with solutions to problems much more quickly. And if that wasn't enough, it has also highlighted the fact that they don't find it as difficult to make new friends compared to other children.

The ability to speak more than one language certainly opened up a lot of possibilities for *me* and I also had a wide range of career choices. But it came as no surprise to many people when I announced I was going into teaching languages. Nowadays I teach students from all over the world and feel so privileged to be part of *their* learning journey.

10 In paragraph 1, what does the writer say about learning languages?

A   Practising a language online is the best way to improve. ☐

B   The skills that are really difficult to improve are reading and listening. ☐

C   Some aspects of languages may be harder for adults than they are for children. ☐

[1]

11 The writer mentions a record with Russian songs to

A   demonstrate how important determination is ☐

B   suggest the quality of the record was not very good ☐

C   explain who her favourite artist was at the time. ☐

[1]

12 What influenced the writer's decision to study abroad?

A   She wanted to have a similar experience to one of her relatives. ☐

B   She felt her English lessons at school were not right for her. ☐

C   She was keen to prove to others she was an independent person. ☐

[1]

13 What does 'it' in line 36 refer to?

A   the start of a very exciting journey ☐

B   the decision to learn more languages ☐

C   coming to Switzerland for a holiday. ☐

[1]

> **TIP**
>
> For the option to be correct, the idea in the option needs to fully match the idea in the text. In this exercise, this applies to Questions 10, 11, 12 and 14.

14 In paragraph 4, we learn that

    A children who can speak more than one language are better at solving things ☐

    B there is a lot of research being done into the benefits of being bilingual ☐

    C the writer regrets not starting to learn foreign languages earlier in life. ☐

                                                       [1]

15 The writer's main reason for writing this blog was to highlight

    A the importance of having a good teacher ☐

    B the importance of learning foreign languages ☐

    C the importance of being bilingual for people's careers. ☐

                                                        [1]

                                                      [Total: 6]

Language focus

After you have answered all the questions in Exercise 4, look at the **Language focus** box following each question. These boxes contain guidance that will help you focus on the important vocabulary and grammar that you need to select the correct answer. Then read the text again to check if you selected the correct answers the first time.

10 In paragraph 1, what does the writer say about learning languages?

    A Practising a language online is the best way to improve.

    B The skills that are really difficult to improve are reading and listening.

    C Some aspects of languages may be harder for adults than they are for children.

LANGUAGE FOCUS 10

Look at the highlighted key detail for each option A–C.

What does the writer say about each of these highlighted ideas in the text in paragraph 1? Does the information in the text match the whole idea in each option?

Which is the correct option? Why are the other options wrong?

---

11 The writer mentions a record with Russian songs to

    A demonstrate how important determination is

    B suggest the quality of the record was not very good

    C explain who her favourite artist was at the time.

LANGUAGE FOCUS 11

Look at the highlighted key detail for each option A–C.

What does the writer say about each of these highlighted ideas in the text in paragraph 1? Does the information in the text match the whole idea in each option?

Which is the correct option? Why are the other options wrong?

---

12 What influenced the writer's decision to study abroad?

    A She wanted to have a similar experience to one of her relatives.

    B She felt her English lessons at school were not right for her.

    C She was keen to prove to others she was an independent person.

LANGUAGE FOCUS 12

Look at the highlighted key detail for each option A–C.

Which of the three options made the writer decide to study abroad? Read carefully what the writer says about each of these highlighted ideas in the text in paragraph 2.

Does the information in the text match the whole idea in each option?

Which is the correct option? Why are the other options wrong?

---

13 What does 'it' in line 36 refer to?

    A the start of a very exciting journey

    B the decision to learn more languages

    C coming to Switzerland for a holiday.

LANGUAGE FOCUS 13

Look at the end of paragraph 3. Does the pronoun 'it' refer to the idea that comes before it or after it?

Which idea is likely to continue (i.e. is like a journey)?

---

14 In paragraph 4, we learn that

    A children who can speak more than one language are better at solving things

    B there is a lot of research being done into the benefits of being bilingual

    C the writer regrets not starting to learn foreign languages earlier in life.

LANGUAGE FOCUS 14

Look at the highlighted key detail for each option A–C.

Read carefully what the writer says about each of these highlighted ideas in the text in paragraph 4?

Does the information in the text match the whole idea in each option?

Which is the correct option? Why are the other options wrong?

15 The writer's main reason for writing this blog was to highlight

    A the importance of having a good teacher

    B the importance of learning foreign languages

    C the importance of being bilingual for people's careers.

LANGUAGE FOCUS 15

Think why the writer wrote this blog. What is the message the writer wanted to communicate to the reader? Quickly look through all the paragraphs again. Is the idea from each option implied in most paragraphs, or only in one or two paragraphs?

When you have finished doing this part of the test and the **Language focus** section, go to the answer key for Section 1, Unit 1.3 and check your answers.

Your score:....................... out of 6

CHECK YOUR PROGRESS

Now think about your progress so far and answer the following questions:

- Did you remember to use all the exam techniques you learnt in Unit 1.2, Exercise 4?

- Was your score in Exercise 4 in this unit better or worse than your scores in Exercise 4 in Unit 1.2? Why do you think this is?

- After doing the **Language focus** sections for this part of the exam, did you find it easier to find the correct answers? Are you now better at recognising what the correct opinion is and what the distracting information is?

- What do you still find difficult? What are you going to do to improve this?

Test 3

Exercise 5

16 You recently met someone new.

Write an email to a friend about the person.

In your email, you should:

- describe how you met

- explain why you like them

- say what you are looking forward to doing with them next.

Write about 120 to 160 words.

You will receive up to 6 marks for the content of your email, and up to 9 marks for the language.

[Total: 15]

When you have finished doing this part of the test, look at the model answer that follows. Read it and compare the content and language used in this email with your email. Then look at the simplified mark scheme in the **What are the examiners looking for?** section, in Unit 1.2. Try to guess what mark you might get for the content and language in your email.

Your score for content:...................... out of 6

Your score for language:...................... out of 9

Model answer

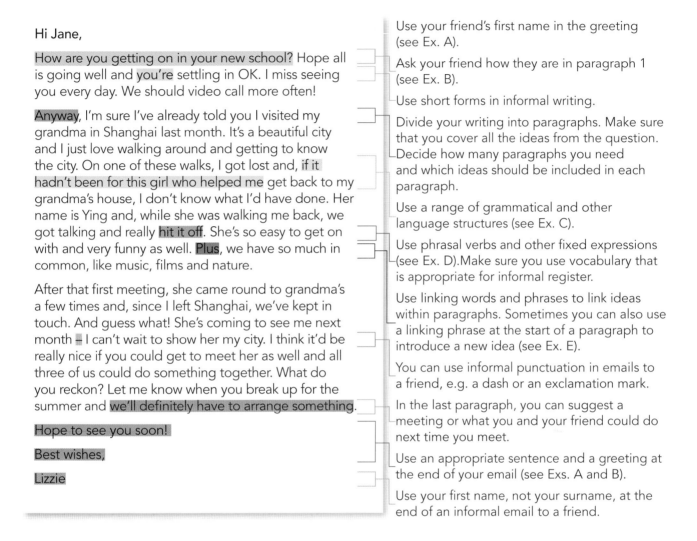

Hi Jane,

How are you getting on in your new school? Hope all is going well and you're settling in OK. I miss seeing you every day. We should video call more often!

Anyway, I'm sure I've already told you I visited my grandma in Shanghai last month. It's a beautiful city and I just love walking around and getting to know the city. On one of these walks, I got lost and, if it hadn't been for this girl who helped me get back to my grandma's house, I don't know what I'd have done. Her name is Ying and, while she was walking me back, we got talking and really hit it off. She's so easy to get on with and very funny as well. Plus, we have so much in common, like music, films and nature.

After that first meeting, she came round to grandma's a few times and, since I left Shanghai, we've kept in touch. And guess what! She's coming to see me next month – I can't wait to show her my city. I think it'd be really nice if you could get to meet her as well and all three of us could do something together. What do you reckon? Let me know when you break up for the summer and we'll definitely have to arrange something.

Hope to see you soon!

Best wishes,

Lizzie

Use your friend's first name in the greeting (see Ex. A).

Ask your friend how they are in paragraph 1 (see Ex. B).

Use short forms in informal writing.

Divide your writing into paragraphs. Make sure that you cover all the ideas from the question. Decide how many paragraphs you need and which ideas should be included in each paragraph.

Use a range of grammatical and other language structures (see Ex. C).

Use phrasal verbs and other fixed expressions (see Ex. D).Make sure you use vocabulary that is appropriate for informal register.

Use linking words and phrases to link ideas within paragraphs. Sometimes you can also use a linking phrase at the start of a paragraph to introduce a new idea (see Ex. E).

You can use informal punctuation in emails to a friend, e.g. a dash or an exclamation mark.

In the last paragraph, you can suggest a meeting or what you and your friend could do next time you meet.

Use an appropriate sentence and a greeting at the end of your email (see Exs. A and B).

Use your first name, not your surname, at the end of an informal email to a friend.

Language focus

Read the model answer again and look at the comments. These comments give you information about important features needed when you write an email to a friend. Did you include these features in your own email? If not, or if you find any of the things mentioned in the comments difficult, go to the appropriate exercise in this **Language focus** section to practise them.

Exercise A: Opening and closing greetings

Look at the following greetings and put them under the correct heading in one of the three tables.

> **Hi there,**   Love,   Yours sincerely,   Hi Fiona,   **Dear John,**
> **All the best,**   **Dear Ms Henderson,**   **Regards,**
> To whom it may concern: Dear Sir/Madam,   **Best wishes,**
> **Kind regards,**   Yours faithfully,   Cheers,

Informal (a friend, or someone you know very well, e.g. your sister or cousin)

Opening greetings	Closing greetings

Semi-formal (someone you know, but who is not a close friend, e.g. your football coach)

Opening greetings	Closing greetings

Formal (someone you do not know at all, or someone who you need to show respect to, e.g. your teacher, someone you want to invite to your school for a talk)

Opening greetings	Closing greetings

Exercise B: Fixed expressions commonly used in opening and closing paragraphs

a   Look at the sentences in the following table containing common fixed expressions. We often use them when we write to a friend, or someone we know very well. Think about their meaning and why we use them. Then match them to their correct function on the left.

TIP

Be careful which greeting you choose. First think who you are writing to and how well you know this person. Then decide how formal your greeting and the rest of the writing should be. The language you use depends on how formal your writing needs to be.

TIP

Only use the greeting 'Yours faithfully,' if you do not know the name of the person you are writing to. When you know the name, use 'Yours sincerely,' instead.

Functions		Common fixed expressions	
A	To ask someone how they are or how they are coping with something (used in the opening paragraph)	1	Hope to see you soon.
		2	How are you doing?
		3	I've got to apologise about last time. The reason why I didn't phone was that I'd lost your number. Sorry about that.
B	To apologise for something and give an explanation (used in the opening paragraph)	4	How about coming with me to see the new movie tomorrow?
		5	Sorry about last time. I didn't mean to upset you.
C	To invite somebody to meet you or to do something with you (used in the closing paragraph)	6	Can't wait to see you again.
		7	How are things with you and your family?
		8	Hope you're not angry with me for not writing to you for so long.
D	To say that you are excited about something that is going to happen (used in the closing paragraph)	9	Fancy coming to my party on Saturday?
		10	Looking forward to going skating with you next week.
		11	Sorry for taking so long with my answer, but I've been very busy at school.
E	To ask what your friend thinks about something (used in the closing paragraph)	12	What do you reckon?
		13	How are you getting on with your exams?
		14	Let me know which one you prefer.

> **TIP**
>
> These fixed expressions will make your email to a friend sound more natural.

b   Now complete the following sentences with your own ideas.

1   How are you getting on with ....?

  Example: How are you getting on with your school project?

2   How are things ....?

3   Sorry for ...., but ....

  ....?

4   Hope you're not angry with me for ....

  ....

5   Fancy ....?

6   Let me know ....

7   Looking forward to ....

8   Can't wait to ....

Exercise C: Language structures

a Read Test 3 Exercise 5 again and then look at the model answer. Can you find structures that are used to answer each of the bullet points from the exam? Write the structures under the correct bullet point in this exercise.

- Describe how you met.

    Example: *I got lost* …

    ....

    ....

    ....

    ....

    ....

- Explain why you like them.

    Example: *She's so easy to get on with* …

    ....

    ....

- Say what you are looking forward to doing with them next.

    Example: *I think it'd be really nice if you could get to meet her as well…*

    ....

    ....

    ....

b Now use the language structures from the model answer, or other structures you know, to talk about the following points:

1 Describe how you met your best friend.

2 Describe your journey to school this morning.

3 Describe what happened on your holiday.

4 Explain why you like your best friend.

5 Explain why you like one of your teachers.

6 Explain why you do not like a character in a film you have seen recently.

7 Say what you are looking forward to doing with your best friend this weekend.

8 Say what you are looking forward to doing on your next holiday.

9 Say what you are looking forward to doing when you grow up.

Exercise D: Phrasal verbs and other fixed expressions

Look at the phrasal verbs and fixed expressions in the following table. They are taken from the model answer. Read the model answer again and try to guess the meaning of these phrasal verbs and fixed expressions. Then match the correct meaning (1–8) to each phrasal verb and fixed expression (A–H).

Phrasal verbs and fixed expressions		Meanings	
A	How are you getting on …?	1	We started chatting.
B	… getting to know the city	2	It is easy to be with this person because they are very easy-going.
C	We got talking …	3	How are you coping?
D	We hit it off	4	to stay in contact via phone or email
E	She's so easy to get on with	5	students finish their classes at the end of the term to start their holidays
F	She came round to grandma's	6	What is your opinion?
G	We've kept in touch	7	to become friends with someone quickly and easily
H	What do you reckon?	8	to discover more information about a place and to become more familiar with it
I	… when you break up for the summer	9	to come to somebody's house for a visit

Exercise E: Linking ideas together using appropriate linking words and phrases

a   Look at the model answer again and find the linking words and phrases used in the email. Then put each of them in one of the following categories. Remember to copy the whole sentence, not just the word or phrase.

- Adding information

   ....

   ....

   ....

   ....

   ....

   ....

TIP

Some phrasal verbs have more than one meaning (e.g. *break up*). That is why you should learn them in context, not on their own. This will help you to understand the meaning and how the verb is used.

TIP

Most phrasal verbs in English are informal. This means you should use them when you are talking or writing to a friend. They are not usually suitable for more formal occasions, such as job interviews or formal essays.

TIP

If you do not use any linking words and phrases, your writing will not sound natural or fluent. It may also be difficult for the reader to follow the ideas in your writing.

- Saying when something happens/happened

....

....

....

....

- Giving an example

....

- Changing the topic / starting a new topic

....

- Giving surprising news

....

b Now look at the sentences you copied in Exercise **a** and study how the linking words and phrases are used. Then use them to talk, or write, about the following topics:

1 Talk about all the things you did last weekend and say when you did these things.

Example: I had a lot of homework, so I spent Sunday afternoon doing just that. While I was looking for some information online, I came across a very useful website. Plus, on Sunday evening, we had some guests over, so I had to help out with the dinner.

2 Say if you enjoy sports and give examples.

3 Talk about something surprising that has happened to you.

4 Talk about what you are doing this week and, then, about your future plans for the next few years.

TIP

In emails to a friend, make sure that you use linking words and phrases that are appropriate for the register. Linking phrases like 'moreover' or 'for instance' are too formal and, therefore, inappropriate for this style of writing.

Learn from mistakes

a Before you rewrite the first draft of your email, look at the following exercise. It includes one student's answer to Exercise 5 in Test 3. Read the student's email and then complete the following table. Decide how well the student did in each area and put a tick in the appropriate box. The first one has been done for you as an example.

New message

← → ↻

Dear Lucie,

Hope you're doing well, Thank you for your email. I'm fine, and I'm enjoying my new school and life in Birmingham.

I've met many brilliant people. In particular, I get on well with one girl. The first time we met each other was funny! I was in the queue in the school canteen and I started to talk with one girl. After we sat down at the same table and she introduced me to her friend, Simona. Simona and I discovered we had a lots of in common, for example we both like going to the cinema! So, we decided to keep in touch. And now we often go out together and we organised many activities.

That reminds me, our friendship. She's like you – very easy-going and interesting in everything. This may surprise you, but I've already planned activities till the end of the August. You know, I've never did such a thing before! As a consequence, my agenda has plenty of appointments.

I hope you can come to visit me here next month so I can introduce you to her. I can't wait to see you again.

Love,

Valerie

Send

How well did the student do in the following areas?	Very well	OK, some improvement still needed	Poorly, a lot of improvement needed
All points from the question are covered		✓	
The included ideas are relevant			
All three points from the question are well developed			
The format is appropriate (i.e. email)			
The register is appropriate (i.e. informal)			
The email is of the correct length			
The ideas are organised into paragraphs			
The ideas are linked with a range of linking words and phrases			

How well did the student do in the following areas?	Very well	OK, some improvement still needed	Poorly, a lot of improvement needed
There's a wide range of vocabulary			
There's a wide range of grammatical structures			
There are very few mistakes and the meaning is always clear			

b   Now look at the same email again. Some of the more serious mistakes in grammar and vocabulary have been highlighted by a teacher. What type of mistakes are they? Can you correct them?

New message

← → ⟳

Dear Lucie,

Hope you're doing well, Thank you for your email. I'm fine, and I'm enjoying my new school and life in Birmingham.

I've met many brilliant people. ¹In particular, I get on well with one girl. The first time we met each other was funny! I was in the queue in the school canteen and I started to talk with one girl. ²After we sat down at the same table and she introduced me to her friend, Simona. Simona and I discovered we had ³a lots of in common, for example we both like going to the cinema! So, we decided to keep in touch. And now we often go out together and we ⁴organised many activities.

⁵That reminds me, our friendship. She's like you – very easy-going and ⁶interesting in everything. This may surprise you, but I've already planned activities till the end of ⁷the August. You know, I've never ⁸did such a thing before! ⁹As a consequence, my ¹⁰agenda has plenty of appointments.

I hope you can come to visit me here next month so I can introduce you to her. I can't wait to see you again.

Love,

Valerie

▾ | 📎 ☐ 🔍   **Send**

---

c   Now you are ready to rewrite the first draft of your email and try to improve it. When you are rewriting your email, remember everything you have learnt in the **Language focus** and **Learn from mistakes** sections. When you have finished writing your second draft, decide if it is better than your first draft. What marks do you think you would get for your second draft?

Your score for content:..................... out of 6

Your score for language:..................... out of 9

CHECK YOUR PROGRESS

Now think about your progress so far and answer the following questions:

- When you were writing your email, did you remember to use all the exam techniques you learnt in Unit 1.2, Exercise 5?

- When you were writing your second draft, did you remember to use the language features that you learnt about in Exercise 5 in this unit?

- Was your score in Exercise 5 in this unit better or worse than your score in Exercise 5 in Unit 1.2? Why do you think this is?

- After doing the **Learn from mistakes** section in this unit, do you now know which areas of your own writing you are good at and which ones you need to improve?

- Is there anything that you still find difficult? What are you going to do to improve this?

Test 3

Exercise 6

17 You have just finished reading a book that your friend gave you for your birthday. You found out that a few other students read the same book so you discussed it together. You now decide to write a review of the book for your school magazine.

In your review, say what the book is about and whether you would recommend it to others.

Here are some comments from other students:

TIP

In the exam, you could also be asked to write a review of a film, a website, a restaurant, a concert, etc. Your review should inform, but also entertain, so it should **not** be too formal.

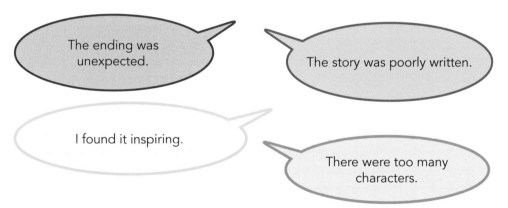

The ending was unexpected.

The story was poorly written.

I found it inspiring.

There were too many characters.

Now write a review of the book for your school magazine.

The comments above may give you some ideas, and you should also use some ideas of your own.

Write about 120 to 160 words.

You will receive up to 6 marks for the content of your review, and up to 9 marks for the language used.

[Total: 15]

When you have finished doing this part of the test, look at the model answer that follows. Read it and compare the content and language used in this review with your review. Then look at the simplified mark scheme in the **What are the examiners looking for?** section. Try to guess what mark you might get for the content and language in your review.

Your score for content:......................... out of 6

Your score for language:......................... out of 9

1 Introduce the book in the opening paragraph (see Ex. A).

2 Introduce the plot in the middle paragraph, but don't describe the whole story.

3 Use the present simple tense when describing the plot.

4 Use a range of adjectives to describe the characters (see Ex. B).

5 Don't tell the reader how the story ends.

Model answer

[1]*The Woman in White* is a mystery novel by Wilkie Collins, published in 1859. The story, set in 19th-century England, revolves around five characters – an art teacher called Walter Hartright, two half-sisters Mariam and Laura, the villain Sir Percival and the mysterious woman in white.

[2]At the start of the story, the ghostly figure of a woman dressed in white appears to Walter. She tries to tell him something before he departs for Cumberland, in north-west England, to start a job as a private art teacher. When he arrives in Cumberland, [3]he's surprised that one of his students, Laura, is very similar to the woman in white. Laura and Walter fall in love, but can't stay together because Laura is to be married to Sir Percival, a cruel and dishonest [4]man who also hides a terrible secret.[5]

[6]What is the secret? Who is the woman in white and what is she trying to warn Walter about? These questions keep readers guessing. However, when I first read the book, I felt [7]like giving up after the first few pages, which would have been a mistake. [8]This was just Collins' clever way of making readers wait before unfolding the gripping mystery. [9]Behind the story, the readers also uncover the truth about the morals of Victorian England. It's definitely well worth reading.[10]

6 Keep the reader interested in your review (e.g. ask questions).

7 In the final paragraph, say what you thought of the book when you were reading it (see Ex. C).

8 Explain why you would or wouldn't recommend the book.

9 Use a range of adjectives to support your opinion of the book (see Ex. B).

10 Summarise your opinion and give your recommendation (see Ex. C).

TIP
When you write a review of a place (e.g. a museum) or an event (e.g. a concert) you should: 1 introduce the place/event   2 say what happened when you were there   3 say whether you would recommend the place/event to others, and why.

Language focus

Read the model answer again and look at the comments. These comments give you information about important features needed when you write a review. Did you include these features in your own review? If not, or if you find any of the things mentioned in the comments difficult, go to the appropriate exercise in this **Language focus** section to practise them.

Exercise A: Introductory information (opening paragraph)

Look at the following phrases. They can be used in the opening paragraph of a book or film review. First, decide what type of information goes in each gap. Then complete the gaps with information about a book or a film you know and write a short introductory paragraph.

1   It is set in .... during ....

2   It has received ....

3   It was written / directed by... .

4   It takes place on .... / in ....

5   It is about ....

6   It is a ....

> **TIP**
>
> You do not have to use all of these phrases in the opening paragraph. Keep the introduction short.

Exercise B: Adjectives (middle and last paragraphs)

a   Look at the following adjectives and decide if they have a positive or negative meaning. Then decide if we use them to describe the plot, characters or the author of a book and put the adjectives in the correct box in the following table. Some of the adjectives can be used to describe more than one thing.

> **gripping**   clever   far-fetched   original   **inspirational**   likeable
> **dull**   **creative**   touching   absorbing   imaginative   **entertaining**
> believable   **talented**   **slow-paced**   **confusing**   witty   **dreadful**
> realistic   deceitful

Category	Adjectives	
	Positive	Negative
The plot		
The characters		
The author		

b   Now think of a book you have read or a film you have seen, and use the adjectives to write a few sentences to say something about the plot, the main characters and the author / the director.

Exercise C: Personal opinion and recommendations (final paragraph)

a   The phrases in the following table can be used to say what you think about a book or a film. Can you match the correct halves together? Which of these phrases would you use to say whether you enjoyed or didn't enjoy the book / film?

1	If I were you,	A	put the book down. It's a real page-turner.
2	I was sitting	B	will enjoy it, but for me it was a real let-down.
3	I couldn't	C	I was this impressed.

> **TIP**
>
> Your review can be positive, negative or a combination of both. If you are writing a review of a place or an event, your opinion/recommendation in the final paragraph should match the information you give in the middle paragraph.

4	I'd definitely recommend	D	miss the chance to see / read this one. It's thoroughly enjoyable.
5	I suppose people who like this genre	E	I wouldn't waste my money on this.
6	It's been a long time since	F	on the edge of my seat throughout the entire film.
7	You definitely shouldn't	G	bored in my life. Avoid at all costs.
8	I've never been so	H	reading this novel. It's worth every penny.

b   Watch a few trailers of the latest films online. Then use the appropriate phrases to write a short paragraph to say what you think of them and whether you would recommend them to others, and why.

Learn from mistakes

a   Before you rewrite the first draft of your review, look at the following exercise. It includes one student's answer to Exercise 6 in Test 3. Read the student's review and then complete the following table. Decide how well the student did in each area and put a tick in the appropriate box. The first one has been done for you as an example.

How well did the student do in the following areas?	Very well	OK, some improvement still needed	Poorly, a lot of improvement needed
The points from the question are covered (i.e. what the book is about, a recommendation)		✓	
The included ideas are relevant			
All ideas are well developed			
The format is appropriate (i.e. a review)			
The register is appropriate (i.e. semi-formal)			
The review is of the correct length			
The ideas are organised into paragraphs			
The ideas are linked with a range of linking words and phrases			

There's a wide range of vocabulary			
There's a wide range of grammatical structures			
There are very few mistakes and the meaning is always clear			

I would like to introduce a book which is called *007 Goldfinger*. About the plot, the whole story was tense and exciting. We can see James Bond how he solved so many crises again and again. It was really entertaining. I believe that readers will can not to continue to read it!

Needless to say, the characters' personality are also important for a story. The main actor James Bond was loyal and clever, in this book, although James Bond was captured by the villain Goldfinger. However, James never gave up or betrayed his country. Furthermore, just like a detective, he could notice details that normal people could not. As for Goldfinger, he had a lot of resources to use to do lots of bad things. Also, Goldfinger was not smart, he was fooled by James Bond many times, which is funny for readers.

Nowadays, audiences can see many modern 007 movie adaptations, but sometimes they are too commercial. We can find 007 books more origin.

b   Now look at the same review again. Some of the more serious mistakes in grammar and vocabulary have been highlighted by a teacher. What type of mistakes are they? Can you correct them?

I would like to introduce a book which is called 007 Goldfinger. About the plot, the whole story was tense and exciting. We can see James Bond [1]how he [2]solved so many crises again and again. It was really entertaining. I believe that readers [3]will can not to continue to read it!

Needless to say, the characters' [4]personality are also important for a story. The main [5]actor James Bond [6]was loyal and clever, in this book, [7]although James Bond was captured by the villain Goldfinger. However, James never gave up or betrayed his country. [8]Furthermore, just like a detective, he [9]could notice details that normal people [10]could not. As for Goldfinger, he [11]had a lot of resources to use to do lots of bad things. Also, Goldfinger [12]was not smart, he [13]was fooled by James Bond many times, which is funny [14]for readers.

Nowadays, audiences can see many modern 007 movie adaptations, but sometimes they are too commercial. We can [15]find 007 books more [16]origin.

c   Read the review again. Use the existing ideas from the review and decide how you would group them together into paragraphs. Also think about how you could develop the introduction and the recommendations better. Then rewrite the review to improve it. When you finish your review, compare it with the example in the answer key for Section 1, Unit 1.3.

d   Now you are ready to rewrite the first draft of your review and try to improve it. When you are rewriting your review, remember everything you have learnt in the **Language focus** and **Learn from mistakes** sections. When you have finished writing your second draft, decide if it is better than your first draft. What marks do you think you would get for your second draft?

> Your score for content:...................... out of 6
>
> Your score for language:...................... out of 9

CHECK YOUR PROGRESS

Now think about your progress so far and answer the following questions:

*   When you were writing the second draft of your review, did you remember to use the language features that you learnt about in Exercise 6 in this unit?

*   After doing the **Learn from mistakes** section in this unit, do you now know which areas of your own writing you are good at and which ones you need to improve?

*   Is there anything that you still find difficult? What are you going to do to improve this?

For more exam practice go to Unit 1.4.

Unit 1.4: Test yourself

Test 4

Exercise 1

Read the article about the history of the Gold Rush and an expedition inspired by the original Gold Rush, and then answer the questions.

The Gold Rush

Before the Gold Rush, the Klondike region in the north-west of Canada was just wilderness. There was little more than a tiny camp built for fishermen, who came every year to fish for salmon. That all changed with the discovery of gold in 1896. It was this year that saw the beginning of what became known as the Klondike Gold Rush. However, this was not the first Gold Rush in North America. The Gold Rush in California, for example, started much earlier – in 1848 in fact.

After the news became public, many people gave up their jobs to go and look for gold and wealth. It is believed that as many as 100,000 people decided to make this extremely long and dangerous journey. However, a lack of experience in coping with such extreme conditions meant that many turned back. Finding gold wasn't easy and, out of the 30,000 who made it all the way, only 4,000 were lucky enough to find some gold. To accommodate all the new arrivals, so-called boom towns started to appear all over the place. One example of such a town was Dawson City, often just referred to as the city that never slept. However, after the Gold Rush was over in 1899, all these places went into decline.

The Gold Rush era has inspired many people. Steve Daniels, a historian, decided to make a documentary about it called *Expedition Gold Rush*. He put a team together and decided to retrace the steps of the original gold seekers and relive their experiences. Before reaching Canada, they first had the risky task of crossing the mountains in Alaska.

Once the team got to the Yukon River, Steve decided that they would build a boat themselves following some of the original designs. They managed to build it after a lot of effort, but the boat didn't look very safe, something that another team member was rather concerned about. Steve, however, thought it was solid enough to take them down the river and this created a bit of tension between the two. In the end, the whole team agreed to travel in the boat. During the night the team slept in tents on the river bank where they had a nasty shock in the morning, when they had a close encounter with a grizzly bear. Their rowing skills were also tested to the limit during a sudden storm.

When they finally reached their destination, the team were exhausted, but said they'd had an enjoyable time. They all agreed there were moments that made them question whether they wanted to continue, like climbing steep icy rocks. However, the stunning scenery more than made up for everything.

1 When did the Klondike Gold Rush begin?

.... [1]

2 How many people arrived in the Klondike region during the Gold Rush?

.... [1]

3 What were the new towns in the Klondike region known as?

.... [1]

4 What did Steve Daniels and one of the members of the expedition disagree about?

.... [1]

5 What did the members of the expedition enjoy most during their journey?

.... [1]

6 What dangerous situations did the members of Expedition Gold Rush experience? Give **three** details.

....

....

.... [3]

[Total: 8]

> When you have finished doing this part of the test, go to the answer key for Section 1, Unit 1.4 and check your answers.
>
> Your score:.................. out of 8

Exercise 2

Read the magazine article about four people (**A–D**) who talk about books they have recently read. Then answer Question **7**.

What do you think of the book you have recently read?

A Alicia

I love reading. Ever since I learnt to read, books have been an important part of my life and they often help me relax and even give me inspiration from time to time. When I'm reading, it feels like I can become someone else for a while. When I was growing up, I was a bit of a tomboy, pretending I was an adventurer exploring foreign lands. This was also reflected in my choice of reading material.

I was never one for love stories until my friend made me read one. I gave it a go, not expecting much of it, but it actually turned out to be a well-written story. Normally, I would hate having more than a handful of main characters, but not here. Somehow, all the characters fitted well in the story. Nevertheless, the author saved the best for last with a conclusion I didn't see coming. Some people say it might even be shortlisted for the National Best Read Prize.

B Ben

I read a lot. People often wonder how I manage to read so much, but my job involves travelling, so I have time to read on the train or while waiting for a flight. The last book I read was a real-life story about a man who relocates to a new country to start over. I generally enjoy this genre because the stories are so inspiring, but I was surprised what a let-down this one was. I don't think the writer did much research on what happens in real life and it certainly didn't convince me. The book was generally an easy read, but at times I got lost because of all the names. I found myself going back to check who was who. However, it wouldn't surprise me if this book got picked by the critics as their favourite in the Brontë Sisters Competition. It often seems to me that critics tend to praise books that I don't enjoy.

C Carla

Unlike many of my friends, I don't read a lot. That's not to say I don't read at all, but the only time I can read is during my summer holidays. I look at the books that have received some awards, or are recommended by other readers, before I choose one, just as I did with the last book. At first, I thought I'd made a mistake with my choice. It was a novel set in France, in the 1940s, an era which I love, but the story included these long philosophical passages. They were quite hard to get through, but I stuck at it because I was

eager to find out what happened to the main heroine. One of my friends couldn't believe I liked this kind of story, but when I was reading about the main character's life, I found myself thinking how similar it was to mine. In the end, it even gave me the idea of visiting France and learning French.

D Dabir

I expect to learn something new from books, to give me new ideas. For this reason, I often go for non-fiction titles. This doesn't mean, however, that I avoid fiction altogether. I finished reading one novel just last week. It was advertised as one of the best novels of the year by an upcoming author – and one that the whole family will thoroughly enjoy. I'm not sure if many teenagers would agree with that statement. When I finished reading it, I had mixed feelings about the book. I thought the storyline had potential because it dealt with the topic of trust and friendship, but I felt the writer could have exploited it a bit more. Nevertheless, the writer clearly spent time researching the characters, who were totally believable. Sometimes I had the feeling that I knew the vast majority of them from real life. I believe that this author shows great promise and, with time, will produce some award-winning titles.

For each question write the correct letter A, B, C or D on the line.

7   Which person…

a   says the book inspired them to do something?   .... [1]

b   suggests the book would benefit from fewer characters?   .... [1]

c   claims the ending was unexpected?   .... [1]

d   says the book reminded them of their own experiences?   .... [1]

e   thinks the book will get an award?   .... [1]

f   doubts if the book is suitable for younger readers?   .... [1]

g   finds most of the characters in the book familiar?   .... [1]

h   is surprised they enjoyed this style of book?   .... [1]

i   says the story was hard to believe?   .... [1]

[Total: 9]

When you have finished doing this part of the test, go to the answer key for Section 1, Unit 1.4 and check your answers.

Your score:...................... out of 9

Exercise 3

Read the article about Mars and Mars preparation projects, and then complete the following notes.

Are we going to Mars soon?

People have always had a desire to explore unknown territories. After the first man landed on the Moon in 1969, people's attention turned to Mars. While going to Mars sounded like a fantasy a few decades ago, it is starting to look more within reach in the 21st century.

Thanks to technological advances, scientists now have more information about Mars, which is, at present, the most comparable planet to Earth. For example, one day on Mars lasts 24 hours, just like the day we are used to, but the Martian year is much longer with 687 days.

95% of the air on Mars consists of carbon dioxide, compared to only 0.04% in our atmosphere. This means the air is unbreathable for humans. Also, when people land on Mars, they will definitely need very effective protection from the high levels of radiation, something we don't have to worry about back home.

A mission to Mars wouldn't be as quick as a journey to the Moon, which took astronauts only four days. It is estimated that it'll take about nine months just to reach the planet. To be able to return to Earth, they will have to wait for the planet to be in a suitable position, which may take between two and three years.

Preparations for future missions have already begun and there have been several projects involved. In 2007, Russia, China and some European countries started a project called Mars 500. This project took four years and focused on people's ability to cope with living in isolation. Six volunteers stayed in a compound for 520 days with very little contact with the outside world. The current record for the longest time spent in space is held at 437 days. This project also tested how isolation affects people's stress levels. It was interesting to see that some volunteers started to avoid their peers and failed to follow their regular exercising routine. Scientists also collected important data on the impact of isolation on sleeping patterns. Four of the volunteers said they had difficulty sleeping at times. Future missions to Mars will also have to think about practical issues like food supplies and how to overcome much lower gravity levels than those we experience on Earth. Mars 500 also assessed food supplements and their effectiveness.

The University of Hawaii carried out another simulation of Mars-like conditions in 2016. This time they focused on the volunteers' ability to live together in a very limited space. A remote station in Antarctica, called Concordia, is another place where similar experiments were performed. The low temperatures in this region can reach -50 °C on average, but this isn't nearly as extreme as the -140 °C on Mars. The highest temperature on Mars can reach 24 °C, which is comparable to Earth and would be ideal for humans.

Scientists hope that, with each new project, we are a small step closer to a trip to Mars.

Imagine you are going to give a talk about Mars and Mars preparation projects to your science class at school. Use words from the article to help you write some notes.

Make short notes under each heading.

8   How Mars is different to Earth

Example: the Martian year is much longer

  • ....

  • ....

  • .... [3]

9   What the Mars preparation projects tested

  • ....

  • ....

  • ....

  • .... [4]

[Total: 7]

When you have finished doing this part of the test, go to the answer key for Section 1, Unit 1.4 and check your answers.

Your score:...................... out of 7

Exercise 4

Read the following blog written by a surfing instructor, and then answer the questions.

All about surfing, with Dave Scott

My name is Dave Scott and I've been surfing ever since I can remember. When I started, I was very lucky because my father was there to teach me. Since then, I've become a surfing instructor myself and have opened up my own school, where I teach surfing enthusiasts how to get the best out of this sport. Now I want to share my experience and knowledge with those of you who are new to surfing, or are still considering whether or not to take it up.

First of all, you have to be absolutely sure that surfing is what you really want to do. I always tell new surfers to read some blogs or talk to experienced surfers. Just like with anything in life, if you're not committed, you won't get the results you're after and your progress will be very slow. And I make this absolutely clear to everyone before the first lesson begins, to avoid any future disappointment. Unfortunately, I often have to tell my students in the very same first lesson that they've bought the wrong surfing gear. Something nobody wants to hear, which leaves them feeling upset because they've wasted their money unnecessarily. The best thing to do is just hire what you need, in case you decide that surfing is not for you after all.

Also, make sure your first surfboard is as big as possible. This ensures that you can surf big waves much more easily.

Plus, if you can find a board with foam, one that's covered with soft material, get it. Most beginners usually have great difficulty standing up for a very long time, so a board with foam will protect you from getting too many bruises when you fall. Depending on where you decide to surf and the temperature of the sea, you might also need a wetsuit to protect you from the cold. There's nothing more annoying than when a surfer gets cold, has to get out of the water and misses out on some really good waves.

Most other equipment is not so essential, apart from one more thing – a surfboard leash. The leash is a length of rope that is attached to the board and the surfer's ankle. Surfers put it over their foot to make sure that they don't get separated from their board in case they fall into the sea. It shouldn't be too short or you might end up hitting yourself on the board. If you have any doubts, I'm sure you can get good suggestions from your local surfing shop.

Before taking your first lesson, you might also consider looking up a few surfing terms online. Not only will you talk like a real surfer, but you'll also be able to understand what your instructors, or other surfers, are talking about. So, for example, if someone talks about a ding, you'll know that it means they've damaged their surfboard. And one more thing – get a head start by learning about surfing etiquette. This is a set of important dos and don'ts that every surfer needs to follow. If you do, you'll be well-equipped for your first lesson and you won't get yourself in trouble with your fellow surfers. So, good luck and I hope you can get straight into the action and enjoy catching some really good waves very soon!

38

10 What do we learn about Dave in paragraph 1?

    A   He is keen to open a school for surfing instructors. ☐

    B   His father got him his first job as an instructor. ☐

    C   The interest in surfing runs in his family. ☐

                                                         [1]

11 Why do many beginners on Dave's course feel unhappy after their first lesson?

    A   They do not come with the right gear. ☐

    B   They make very little progress in the lesson. ☐

    C   They have to pay a lot of money for the course. ☐

                                                         [1]

12 Why does Dave suggest buying a surfboard with a soft surface?

    A   They offer more safety for new surfers. ☐

    B   They help surfers to keep their balance. ☐

    C   They are easier to turn while surfing. ☐

                                                          [1]

13 What does 'it' refer to in line 38?

    A   foot ☐

    B   rope ☐

    C   board ☐

                                                          [1]

14 In the last paragraph, Dave mentions the word 'ding'

    A   to describe a part of a surfboard ☐

    B   to highlight how dangerous surfing can be ☐

    C   to show the type of language used by surfers. ☐

[1]

15 What was Dave's main reason for writing this blog?

    A   to inform surfers about the best equipment available ☐

    B   to give advice to people who are new to surfing ☐

    C   to explain how he first got into surfing himself. ☐

[1]

[Total 6]

> When you have finished doing this part of the test, go to the answer key for Section 1, Unit 1.4 and check your answers.
>
> Your score:...................... out of 6

Exercise 5

16 Recently, you had to make an important decision about something.

Write an email to a friend telling them about the decision.

In your email, you should:

- explain what the decision was

- say who helped you make this decision, and how

- give examples of how this decision will change your life.

Write about 120 to 160 words.

You will receive up to 6 marks for the content of your email, and up to 9 marks for the language.

[Total: 15]

> When you have finished doing this part of the test, go to the answer key for Section 1, Unit 1.4. Read the model answer and compare the content and language used in this email with your email. Then look at the simplified mark scheme in the **What are the examiners looking for?** section in Section 1, Unit 1.2. Try to guess what mark you might get for the content and language in your email.
>
> Your score for content:...................... out of 6
>
> Your score for language:...................... out of 9

Exercise 6

17 In your lesson you were talking about how important it is to do voluntary work. Your teacher has asked you to write an article for a school magazine.

In your article say how easy or difficult it is for young people to do voluntary work and what could be done to encourage more students to get involved in this type of work.

Here are some comments from other students:

> Students are too busy doing their school work.

> Some volunteers could come to school to talk to students.

> Voluntary work could help students with their career choices.

> Some students would have to travel very far to do voluntary work.

Now write an article for your school magazine.

The comments above may give you some ideas, and you should also use some ideas of your own.

Write about 120 to 160 words.

You will receive up to 6 marks for the content of your email, and up to 9 marks for the language.

[Total: 15]

> When you have finished doing this part of the test, go to the answer key for Section 1, Unit 1.4. Read the model answer and compare the content and language used in this email with your email. Then look at the simplified mark scheme in the **What are the examiners looking for?** section in Section 1, Unit 1.3. Try to guess what mark you might get for the content and language in your email.
>
> Your score for content:...................... out of 6
>
> Your score for language:...................... out of 9

Unit 2.1: About the exam

How much do you already know about the format of the Listening exam and what happens during the exam? Can you answer the following questions?

1   How many parts are there in the Listening exam? .... [1]

2   Look at the following table. Can you match each exercise with the correct exam

task? ....

    .... [5]

TIP

If you are new to the Listening exam, first go to Unit 2.4 and look at the complete test to see what each section looks like.

Listening paper		
Exercise 1	A	**Multiple choice: Talk** You listen to a formal talk and complete eight gapped sentences. You choose the correct answer from three options – A, B or C.
Exercise 2	B	**Multiple choice: Interview** You listen to an interview and answer eight questions. You choose the correct answer from three options – A, B or C.
Exercise 3	C	**Multiple matching: Monologues** You listen to six short monologues. You have to choose the correct statement from a selection of eight and match it to the right speaker based on the idea that each speaker expresses.
Exercise 4	D	**Multiple choice: Short extracts** You listen to five short dialogues or monologues, both formal and informal, and answer two questions about each of them. You choose the correct answer from three options – A, B or C.
Exercise 5	E	**Multiple choice: Short extracts, visual prompts** You listen to eight short informal dialogues or monologues and answer one question about each of them. You choose the correct answer from four pictures – A, B, C or D.

3   How long does the whole Listening exam take? .... [1]

4   What is the total number of marks you can get? .... [1]

5   How many times do you hear each part of the Listening exam? .... [1]

6   Should you answer all the questions on the exam paper? .... [1]

7   Do you lose marks if your answer is wrong? .... [1]

8   Can you use a dictionary during the exam? .... [1]

9   Can you ask for the audio recording to be paused during the exam? .... [1]

10 Do you have time to read the questions before each audio recording

starts? .... [1]

11 Do you have time to check your answers during the exam? .... [1]

12 Do you have to transfer your answers onto a separate answer sheet at the end of

the exam? .... [1]

13 Can you use any type of pen you want to indicate your answer? .... [1]

Now go to the answer key for Section 2, Unit 2.1 and check your answers.

Your score: .... out of 17

CHECK YOUR PROGRESS

Was there anything you didn't know about the Listening exam? Now test yourself to see if you can remember everything mentioned in the previous exercise.

Are the following statements true (T) or false (F)? Circle the correct letter for each statement.

1	During the exam, the audio recording can be paused to give you more time to read the questions.	T / F
2	You hear the audio recording for each exercise twice.	T / F
3	In Exercise 1, you should choose the correct answer from three pictures.	T / F
4	In Exercise 2, you listen to four short audio recordings.	T / F
5	In Exercise 2, you answer two questions for each short audio recording that you hear.	T / F
6	In Exercise 3, you complete ten gapped sentences.	T / F
7	In Exercise 3, you choose the correct answer from three options.	T / F
8	In Exercise 4, there is one extra statement that you do not need to use.	T / F
9	In Exercise 5, for each question there are four options to choose from.	T / F
10	The audio recordings in the listening paper can be formal as well as informal.	T / F
11	You should not leave any blank spaces. You should try to answer all the questions.	T / F
12	At the end of the exam, you have to transfer your answers from the question paper onto a separate answer sheet.	T / F

13	You can ask the teacher for extra time at the end of the exam to check your answers.	T / F
14	You can ask the teacher for a dictionary at the end of the exam to check any unknown vocabulary.	T / F
15	You should use a soft pencil to write your answers.	T / F

Now go to the answer key for Section 2, Unit 2.1 and check your answers.

Your score: .... out of 15

Unit 2.2: Exam strategies

First, do the exercise in Test 1 as you would in the real exam. Then look at the **Reflection** section to see some guidance on how to do this type of exercise. Finally, do the same type of exercise in Test 2 to see if you have improved.

Test 1

> **TIP**
>
> You will hear each part of the Listening exam twice. The first time you listen, try to get as many answers as you can. Then check your answers when the audio recording is repeated.

 ## Exercise 1

You will hear eight short audio recordings. For each question, choose the correct answer, **A**, **B**, **C** or **D**, and put a tick (✓) in the appropriate box.

You will hear each audio recording twice.

Now look at Questions **1–8**.

1 What is the boy going to have for lunch today?

A  B  C  D

☐ ☐ ☐ ☐ [1]

> **TIP**
>
> In the Listening exam, there will be distracting information to test your listening for detail. You need to listen to the surrounding information carefully so that you can decide what the correct answer is. For example, in Exercise 1, all four ideas from the pictures will be mentioned in the audio recording, but only one will be the answer to the question.

2 How will the woman get to the airport?

A   B   C   D

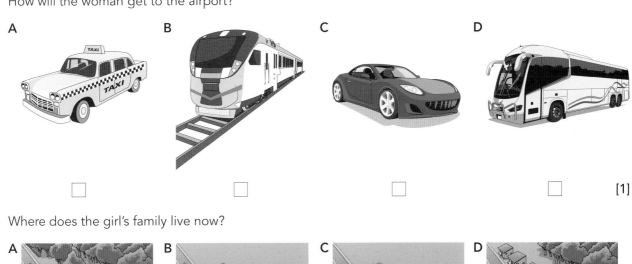

☐   ☐   ☐   ☐   [1]

3 Where does the girl's family live now?

A   B   C   D

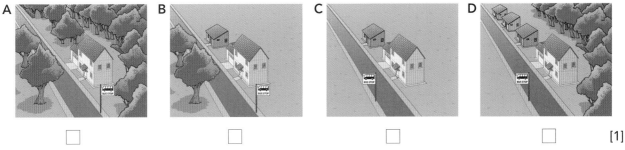

☐   ☐   ☐   ☐   [1]

4 Which jumper does the boy agree to buy?

A   B   C   D

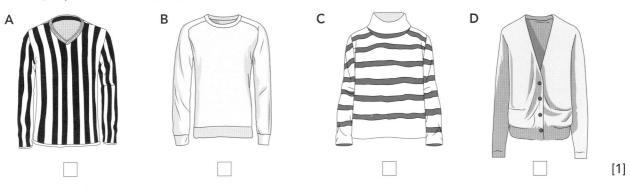

☐   ☐   ☐   ☐   [1]

5 What subject does the girl enjoy most at her new school?

A   B   C   D

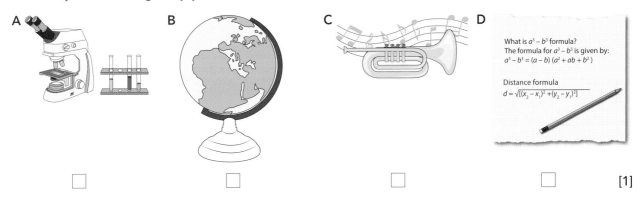

What is $a^3 - b^3$ formula?
The formula for $a^3 - b^3$ is given by:
$a^3 - b^3 = (a - b)(a^2 + ab + b^2)$

Distance formula
$d = \sqrt{[(x_2 - x_1)^2 + (y_2 - y_1)^2]}$

☐   ☐   ☐   ☐   [1]

6 Why was the boy absent from school yesterday?

A 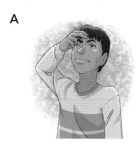 B C D

☐ ☐ ☐ ☐ [1]

7 Where will the taxi driver take the woman to?

A 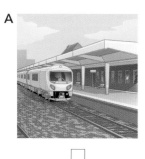 B C D

☐ ☐ ☐ ☐ [1]

8 What was the weather like at the start of the trip?

A 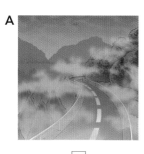 B C D

☐ ☐ ☐ ☐ [1]

[Total: 8]

When you have finished doing this part of the test, go to the answer key for Section 2, Unit 2.2 and check your answers.

Your score: .... out of 8

TIP

After you have checked your answers, look at your mistakes. Listen again to the part of the test where you made a mistake and think about why you made it. Try to avoid making this type of mistake in the future. At the end, you can also read the audioscript to see why you made that mistake.

Reflection

Now think about the way you did Test 1, Exercise 1. Read the questions in the following table and put YES or NO to show you have, or have not, done these things. The questions remind you about the things you should do in Exercise 1 in the Listening exam. If some of your answers are NO, these are the areas you need to practise a bit more to improve your performance in the exam.

Before you started listening	YES or NO	Guidance
1 Did you read the questions carefully before listening?		In this exercise, the audio recording is repeated after each question. This means you do not have to read all eight questions at once, but only one question at a time.
2 Did you highlight the important words in each question?		Remember to highlight important words in questions. This will help you to select the correct detail and avoid the distractors while you are listening.
3 Did you quickly look at the four pictures to see what the options A–D are?		
While you were listening	**YES or NO**	**Guidance**
4 Did you select the correct picture by putting a tick in the box?		If you are unsure which answer is correct after you hear the audio recording for the first time, put a question mark next to the option(s) you think might be the answer. Decide which answer is correct while you are listening for the second time.
After you finished listening	**YES or NO**	**Guidance**
5 Did you choose one option only as your final answer for each question?		If you are still unsure which answer is correct after the audio recording is played the second time, try to guess the answer.
6 Did you write your answers on the question paper only, at this stage?		You will be given **six minutes** at the end of the exam to transfer all your answers onto a **separate answer sheet**. You should not do it during the exam. You should use the time in between exercises to check your answers and read the questions in the next exercise.

If you answered 'No' to any of the questions in the **Reflection** section, try to follow all the guidance from this section when you do Test 2, Exercise 1.

Now do Test 2, Exercise 1.

Test 2

 Exercise 1

You will hear eight short audio recordings. For each question, choose the correct answer, **A**, **B**, **C** or **D**, and put a tick (✓) in the appropriate box.

You will hear each audio recording twice.

Now look at Questions **1–8**.

1 Which activity did the girl enjoy least at the school sports day?

A    B    C    D

☐   ☐   ☐   ☐ [1]

2 What did the boy have to do yesterday?

A    B    C    D

☐   ☐   ☐   ☐ [1]

3 What time does the woman want to meet?

A    B    C    D

☐   ☐   ☐   ☐ [1]

4 Which animal do most students want to research for their presentation?

A 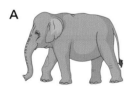   B    C 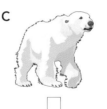   D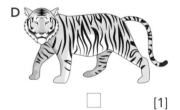

☐   ☐   ☐   ☐ [1]

5 What does the man like most about his new job?

A

B

C

D

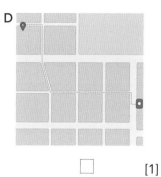

☐   ☐   ☐   ☐   [1]

6 What voluntary work do the friends decide to do?

A

B

C

D

☐   ☐   ☐   ☐   [1]

7 What activity was the girl unable to do during the family trip?

A
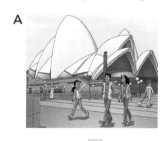

B

C

D

☐   ☐   ☐   ☐   [1]

8 Which school competition has the girl decided to enter this year?

A

B

C

D

☐   ☐   ☐   ☐   [1]

[Total: 8]

CHECK YOUR PROGRESS

Now think about your progress so far and answer the following questions:

- Was your score in Test 2, Exercise 1 higher than in Test 1, or not? Why do you think this is?

- After doing the **Reflection** section for this part of the exam, did you find it easier to do Test 2? What guidance did you find helpful?

- Is there anything that you still find difficult? What are you going to do to improve this?

Develop your skills

In Exercise 1, you listen to short dialogues, monologues, announcements, etc. to test whether you can:

1   understand factual information (e.g. a place, times, free time activities)

2   understand more complex ideas (e.g. speakers' feelings, preferences, decisions)

3   understand how different ideas are connected (e.g. comparing, changing an opinion, ranking).

Try the following activity to improve these listening skills:

- Make a list of question words (e.g. *who, when, what, what time, how much*).

- Listen to a range of audio recordings of different situations (e.g. news headlines, short interviews, public announcements, TV advertisements, songs). You can search for these online.

- Write down correct answers to your question words (e.g. *who – the prime minister; when – yesterday; what – a meeting*).

- Then listen again and write down one or two extra details for each answer (e.g. *the prime minister – visited a school, met the students*).

Test 1

 Exercise 2

You will hear five short audio recordings. For each question, choose the correct answer, **A**, **B** or **C**, and put a tick (✓) in the appropriate box.

You will hear each audio recording twice.

Now look at Questions **9–18**.

You will hear a woman leaving a telephone message for a friend about birthday party preparations.

9 What does the woman offer to help with before the party?

    A   to select the music   ☐

    B   to bake the birthday cake   ☐

    C   to send out the invitations   ☐

    [1]

10 The woman thinks they should hire the community hall because

    A   it does not cost a lot of money   ☐

    B   the location is convenient   ☐

    C   they need a large room.   ☐

    [1]

You will hear two students discussing a talk that they have been to.

11 What was the girl surprised about?

    A   the choice of room   ☐

    B   the number of students   ☐

    C   the lack of breaks   ☐

    [1]

12 What did the students both think of the speaker?

    A   He spoke too quietly.   ☐

    B   He was quite impatient.   ☐

    C   He included unimportant details.   ☐

    [1]

You will hear a man telling his friend about the town centre.

13 Why did the man cycle to the town centre today?

    A   It was an easier way to travel.   ☐

    B   The weather was nice.   ☐

    C   He is trying to get fit.   ☐

    [1]

14 What does the man think of the new shopping centre?

    A   He is disappointed with some of the facilities. ☐

    B   He is critical of the outside of the building. ☐

    C   He is surprised how expensive some shops are. ☐

    [1]

You will hear a man talking about being a restaurant owner.

15 The man says that the hardest part of his job is

    A   dealing with difficult customers ☐

    B   keeping up with the paperwork ☐

    C   finding the right employees. ☐

    [1]

16 What does the man intend to do next?

    A   open another restaurant ☐

    B   improve the menu ☐

    C   provide home delivery ☐

    [1]

You will hear a boy telling his friend about his decision to study abroad.

17 How did the boy's parents react to his decision?

    A   They were worried. ☐

    B   They were surprised. ☐

    C   They were helpful. ☐

    [1]

18 What is the boy looking forward to most about being abroad?

    A   meeting new people ☐

    B   travelling around the country ☐

    C   communicating in another language ☐

    [1]

    [Total: 10]

> When you have finished doing this part of the test, go to the answer key for Section 2, Unit 2.2 and check your answers.
>
> Your score: .... out of 10

Reflection

Now think about the way you did Test 1, Exercise 2. Read the questions in the following table and put YES or NO to show you have, or have not, done these things. The questions remind you about the things you should do in Exercise 2 in the Listening exam. If some of your answers are NO, these are the areas you need to practise a bit more to improve your performance in the exam.

Before you started listening	YES or NO	Guidance
1 Did you read the questions carefully before listening?		In this exercise, the audio recording is repeated after each question. This means you do not have to read all ten questions at once, but only two questions at a time.
2 Did you highlight the important words in each question?		Remember to highlight important words in questions (e.g. *the man, first, next, both, surprised, new*). These will help you select the correct detail and avoid the distractors while you are listening.
3 Did you quickly look what the three options A–C were?		
While you were listening	YES or NO	Guidance
4 Did you match the correct idea from the audio recording to the right option?		The idea in the audio recording will be expressed using different words (either synonyms or paraphrasing) to the words used in the option that is the correct answer. But both ideas will mean the same (e.g. *I was surprised* and *I would never have expected to …*).
5 Did you select the correct option by putting a tick in the box?		If you are unsure which option is the correct answer after you hear the audio recording for the first time, put a question mark next to the option(s) you think might be the answer. Decide which answer is correct while you are listening for the second time.
After you finished listening	YES or NO	Guidance
6 Did you choose one option only as your final answer for each question?		If you are still unsure which answer is correct after the audio recording is played the second time, try to guess the answer.
7 Did you write your answers on the question paper only, at this stage?		You will be given **six minutes** at the end of the exam to transfer all your answers onto a **separate answer sheet**. You should not do it during the exam. You should use the time in between exercises to check your answers and read the questions in the next exercise.

If you answered 'No' to any of the questions in the Reflection section, try to follow all the guidance from this section when you do Test 2, Exercise 2.

Now do Test 2, Exercise 2.

Test 2

 04 Exercise 2

You will hear five short audio recordings. For each question, choose the correct answer, **A**, **B** or **C**, and put a tick (✓) in the appropriate box.

You will hear each audio recording twice.

Now look at questions **9–18**.

You will hear a woman telling a friend about her holidays.

9   What happened to the woman on the first day?

   A   She lost something.   ☐

   B   She made a mistake.   ☐

   C   She had an argument.   ☐

                                                              [1]

10   What did the woman enjoy most about her holiday?

   A   the weather   ☐

   B   the activities   ☐

   C   the landscape   ☐

                                                              [1]

You will hear a girl talking to a friend about her new hobby.

11   How did the girl become interested in baking?

   A   because of social media   ☐

   B   because of her relative   ☐

   C   because of a necessity   ☐

                                                              [1]

12   What surprised the girl most about cake making?

   A   how long the decorating takes   ☐

   B   how expensive the ingredients are   ☐

   C   how many different recipes there are ☐

                                                              [1]

You will hear part of a presentation about the issue of food waste.

13 What does the speaker think causes the most food waste?

    A   inappropriate food storage ☐

    B   large restaurant portions ☐

    C   unnecessary food shopping ☐

    [1]

14 To reduce food waste at home, the speaker suggests

    A   planning weekly meals ☐

    B   checking the quality of food ☐

    C   changing shopping habits. ☐

    [1]

You will hear two friends talking about their school.

15 What does the girl think about the school?

    A   The school gym needs updating. ☐

    B   The school needs new facilities. ☐

    C   The school is too far from her home. ☐

    [1]

16 What are the friends both looking forward to doing?

    A   going on a school trip ☐

    B   taking part in a competition ☐

    C   doing research for their project ☐

    [1]

You will hear a man talking about taking photographs.

17 Why is the man annoyed with his camera?

    A   The size is wrong for him. ☐

    B   The quality of photos is poor. ☐

    C   It is too complicated to use. ☐

    [1]

18 The man prefers taking photos

    A   of moving objects ☐

    B   in a particular location ☐

    C   at certain times of the day. ☐

[1]

[Total: 10]

When you have finished doing this part of the test, go to the answer key for Section 2, Unit 2.2 and check your answers.

Your score: .... out of 10

CHECK YOUR PROGRESS

Now think about your progress so far and answer the following questions:

- Was your score in Test 2, Exercise 2 higher than in Test 1, or not? Why do you think this is?

- After doing the **Reflection** section for this part of the exam, did you find it easier to do Test 2? What guidance did you find helpful?

- Is there anything that you still find difficult? What are you going to do to improve this?

Develop your skills

In Exercise 2, you listen to formal or informal dialogues, parts of interviews or monologues (e.g. instructions, announcements) to test whether you can:

1 understand factual information (e.g. names of places, types of films and free time activities)

2 understand more complex ideas (e.g. speakers' opinions, feelings, preferences, decisions)

3 understand how different ideas are connected (e.g. agreement and disagreement)

4 understand what speakers imply but do not say directly.

Try the following activities to improve these listening skills:

- Listen to a range of dialogues and monologues and write down the main facts the speakers talk about (e.g. the time of arrival, the weather in the morning, their eldest daughter). Then listen again and add more detailed information about each fact (e.g. the weather in the morning was much worse than the speaker expected / the weather forecast for this morning was wrong).

- Listen to online reviews and interviews and write down the topic(s) the speaker talks about (e.g. the film, the acting, the cinema, the special effects). Then listen again and write down what the speaker's opinion is or how they feel about these topics (e.g. he was disappointed, she particularly liked the main hero). Finally, listen one more time to see if they give reasons for their opinions or feelings.

- Listen to a range of dialogues (e.g. interviews with famous people, TV debates, dialogues between two characters in a film). Try to focus on the way they speak, their intonation, the choice of words they use. What do these tell you about the speaker (e.g. they are angry, they are in a hurry, they are happy, they feel embarrassed)?

Improving your knowledge of vocabulary and pronunciation will also help improve your listening skills. The following activities can help you with this.

- After you have listened to this type of listening test, look at the audioscript. Highlight the phrases that paraphrase ideas from the sentences on the question paper (e.g. *taken aback* means the same as *surprised*).

- Listen to formal and informal types of speaking (e.g. speeches, TV debates, dialogues in films). Notice how the choice of words is different in each (e.g. two friends having a chat (informal words), two politicians discussing an issue (formal), your classmate giving a presentation (semi-formal)).

- When you are watching a film, put the subtitles on (but do not do this all the time). Notice what is said/written and how it is pronounced. When we speak in English, some sounds disappear (e.g. *I do not like* becomes *I donlike*), some sounds change (e.g. *handbag* becomes *hambag*) and sometimes there is an extra sound (e.g. *law and order* becomes *lawrand order*).

Test 1

 Exercise 3

You will hear a tour guide called Javier Rodriguez giving a talk about the floating islands on Lake Titicaca in South America. For each question, choose the correct answer, **A**, **B** or **C**, and put a tick (✓) in the appropriate box.

You will hear the talk twice.

Now look at Questions **19–26**.

> **TIP**
>
> The speakers in the exam will have different accents. Try to listen to people from different parts of the world (e.g. the UK, New Zealand, Canada, the USA) speaking in English. This will help you get used to the different way they speak and pronounce their words.

The floating islands on Lake Titicaca

19 Titicaca is the … lake in the world where it is possible to sail.

   A   highest ☐

   B   deepest ☐

   C   largest ☐

   [1]

20 The speaker was surprised local people used a type of grass to make their …

   A   boats ☐

   B   houses ☐

   C   furniture. ☐

   [1]

21 The reed has many benefits but does not offer protection against … in the area.

   A   the humid air ☐

   B   the heavy rain ☐

   C   the strong sun ☐

   [1]

22 The speaker compares the ground of the islands to …

   A   a sinking ship ☐

   B   a slice of cheese ☐

   C   a waterbed. ☐

   [1]

23 Nowadays, the Uros get some money from selling … to the visitors.

   A   fresh fish ☐

   B   traditional clothes ☐

   C   handmade crafts ☐

   [1]

24 The … on the island the speaker went to were different from the ones on other islands.

   A   costumes ☐

   B   dances ☐

   C   songs ☐

   [1]

25 Uros people are only able to eat ... from time to time.

    A   water birds   ☐

    B   potatoes   ☐

    C   eggs   ☐

        [1]

26 The speaker had never expected to find a ... on one of the islands.

    A   motor boat   ☐

    B   solar panel   ☐

    C   radio station   ☐

        [1]

        [Total: 8]

> When you have finished doing this part of the test, go to the answer key for Section 2, Unit 2.2 and check your answers.
>
> Your score: .... out of 8

Reflection

Now think about the way you did Test 1, Exercise 3. Read the questions in the following table and put YES or NO to show you have, or have not done these things. The questions remind you about the things you should do in Exercise 3 in the Listening exam. If some of your answers are NO, these are the areas you need to practise a bit more to improve your performance in the exam.

Before you started listening	YES or NO	Guidance
1 Did you read the statements in each question carefully before listening?		In this exercise, read all eight questions before the audio recording starts. The audio recording is repeated only after the whole talk has finished. The sentences on the question paper appear in the same order as you hear the answers/information in the audio recording.
2 Did you highlight the important words in each sentence?		Remember to highlight important words (e.g. *world, sail*). These will help you to select the correct detail and avoid the distractors while you are listening.
3 Did you quickly look what the three options A–C are?		
While you were listening	**YES or NO**	**Guidance**
4 Did you match the correct idea from the audio recording to the right option?		In Exercise 3, you may hear the three options in the audio recording as they are written in the question (e.g. *deepest – deepest*). But some wording might be different. For example *highest* in the option on the question paper may be worded as *no higher than* in the audio recording.

While you were listening	YES or NO	Guidance
5 Did you select the correct option by putting a tick in the box?		If you are unsure which option is the correct answer after you hear the audio recording for the first time, put a question mark next to the option(s) you think might be the answer. Decide which answer is correct while you are listening for the second time.
After you finished listening	**YES or NO**	**Guidance**
6 Did you choose one option only as your final answer for each question?		If you are still unsure which answer is correct after the audio recording is played the second time, try to guess the answer.
7 Did you write your answers on the question paper only, at this stage?		You will be given **six minutes** at the end of the exam to transfer all your answers onto a **separate answer sheet**. You should not do it during the exam. You should use the time in between exercises to check your answers and read the questions in the next exercise.

If you answered 'No' to any of the questions in the **Reflection** section, try to follow all the guidance from this section when you do Test 2, Exercise 3.

Now do Test 2, Exercise 3.

Test 2

 Exercise 3

You will hear a teacher called Djamila Karim giving a talk about the history and production of chocolate. For each question choose the correct answer, **A**, **B** or **C**, and put a tick (✓) in the appropriate box.

You will hear the talk twice.

Now look at Questions **19–26**.

The story of chocolate

19 The ancient cultures linked to chocolate lived mostly in an area that is now called …

   A Honduras ☐

   B Mexico ☐

   C Guatemala. ☐

   [1]

20 One story claims that after watching the behaviour of … , the Olmecs found out they could eat cocoa beans.

   A toads ☐

   B birds ☐

   C rats ☐

   [1]

21 The speaker was surprised that ancient cultures also added … to their chocolate drinks.

   A herbs ☐

   B spices ☐

   C chillies ☐

   [1]

22 The speaker saw decorations that showed the Mayan people drinking chocolate …

   A after an important event ☐

   B during a celebration ☐

   C at the end of a meal. ☐

   [1]

23 … was the first country in Europe to produce chocolate in the form of a bar.

   A England ☐

   B Spain ☐

   C Switzerland ☐

   [1]

24 For young cocoa trees to grow well, … is particularly important.

    A   shade   ☐

    B   rainfall   ☐

    C   temperature   ☐

    [1]

25 The speaker gives an example of … as one species that has benefited from the change in cocoa farming.

    A   bats   ☐

    B   chimpanzees   ☐

    C   elephants   ☐

    [1]

26 The speaker suggests that eating one type of chocolate can help people with …

    A   their memory   ☐

    B   stomach aches   ☐

    C   blood pressure.   ☐

    [1]

    [Total: 8]

> When you have finished doing this part of the test, go to the answer key for Section 2, Unit 2.2 and check your answers.
>
> Your score: ………… out of 8

CHECK YOUR PROGRESS

Now think about your progress so far and answer the following questions:

- Was your score in Test 2, Exercise 3, higher than in Test 1, or not? Why do you think this is?

- After doing the **Reflection** section for this part of the exam, did you find it easier to do Test 2? What guidance did you find helpful?

- Is there anything that you still find difficult? What are you going to do to improve this?

Develop your skills

In Exercise 3, you listen to a semi-formal talk to test whether you can:

1 understand factual information (e.g. about food, technology, animals, facilities)
2 understand more complex ideas (e.g. speakers' opinions, feelings, experiences)
3 understand how different ideas are connected (e.g. a general feeling versus a personal preference).

You can do the following to improve these listening skills:

A

- Watch documentaries about various topics (e.g. animals, countries, groups of people, buildings, projects). Only watch a short part of around 2–3 minutes.

- Then write down eight words that you hear during this clip that are connected with the topic of the documentary – focus mainly on nouns or numbers (e.g. *lift, 120 metres, office, roof, builders*).

- Finally, listen again to the same clip and write down more detailed information connected to these key words (e.g. *lift – can fit 20 people, 120 metres – the highest block in the city centre*).

B

- Ask someone else to watch a documentary first and then write eight words on eight separate pieces of paper for you.

- Then watch the documentary yourself and put the words in the correct order.

- Watch the documentary again and write some extra details about each word.

C

- Listen to your classmates giving a presentation and take rough notes.

- Then tell your classmates what the presentation was about using your notes.

- Your classmates will listen and tell you what information you got wrong or left out.

Test 1

Exercise 4

You will hear six people talking about shopping. For Questions **27–32**, choose from the list (**A–H**) which idea each speaker expresses. Write the correct letter (**A–H**) on the answer line. Use each letter only once. There are two extra letters that you do not need to use.

You will hear the audio recording twice.

Now read statements **A–H**.

> **TIP**
>
> You will only need to use six of the statements. Two statements are spare.

A	I spend too much when I go shopping.
B	I prefer buying everything online.
C	I rarely buy anything, I just look for inspiration.
D	I do not enjoy shopping, so I try to avoid it.
E	I look for a good price first before buying anything.
F	Going shopping with somebody is a must for me.
G	The way I shop has changed recently.
H	I always plan how much to buy in advance.

27 Speaker 1 .... [1]

28 Speaker 2 .... [1]

29 Speaker 3 .... [1]

30 Speaker 4 .... [1]

31 Speaker 5 .... [1]

32 Speaker 6 .... [1]

[Total: 6]

When you have finished doing this part of the test, go to the answer key for Section 2, Unit 2.2 and check your answers.

Your score: .... out of 6

Reflection

Now think about the way you did Test 1, Exercise 4. Read the questions in the following table and put YES or NO to show you have, or have not, done these things. The questions remind you about the things you should do in Exercise 4 in the Listening exam. If some of your answers are NO, these are the areas you need to practise a bit more to improve your performance in the exam.

Before you started listening	YES or NO	Guidance
1 Did you read the eight statements carefully before listening?		In this exercise, read all eight statements before the audio recording starts. The audio recording is repeated at the end of all six monologues.
		As this is a multiple matching exercise, the statements on the question paper come in a different order to the order the speakers express them in the audio recording.
2 Did you highlight the important words in each statement before listening?		Remember to highlight important words (e.g. *do not enjoy*, *avoid*). These will help you to select the correct idea from the audio recording and avoid the distractors.
While you were listening	**YES or NO**	**Guidance**
3 Did you find the idea in the audio recording that fully matches the statement on the question paper?		Remember that the opinion/idea in the audio recording is always expressed using different words and phrases from the statements on the question paper. Take notes of these words/phrases while you are listening and then match these to the correct statement on the question paper before you listen for the second time.
		Also, watch out for distractors. They are used in the audio recording, in addition to the correct details, to test how accurate your listening skills are. Distractors only express part of the idea, or use one same word, from the statement(s).
4 Did you match as many statements to the speakers as you could during the first listening?		If you cannot decide between two ideas for the same speaker, write both letters on the line. Decide which letter is correct while you are listening for the second time. Do not forget to delete the wrong letter.
5 Did you check your choices for each speaker during the second listening?		
After you finished listening	**YES or NO**	**Guidance**
6 Did you use each letter only once?		If you use the same letter more than once, you may **not** be given any marks for these answers.
7 Did you fill in all six boxes?		If you are still unsure which answer is correct after the audio recording is played the second time, try to guess the answer.
8 Did you write your answers on the question paper only at this stage?		You will be given **six minutes** at the end of the exam to transfer all your answers onto a **separate answer sheet**. You should not do it during the exam. You should use the time in between exercises to check your answers and read the questions in the next exercise.

If you answered 'No' to any of the questions in the **Reflection** section, try to follow all the guidance from this section when you do Test 2, Exercise 4.

Now do Test 2, Exercise 4.

Test 2

Exercise 4

You will hear six people talking about their families. For Questions **27–32**, choose from the list (**A–H**) which idea each speaker expresses. Write the correct letter (**A–H**) on the answer line. Use each letter only once. There are two extra letters that you do not need to use.

You will hear the audio recording twice.

Now read statements **A–H**.

| A | I keep in touch with my family regularly. |

| B | I did not used to get on with some of my relatives. |

| C | I love getting together for special occasions. |

| D | In the past, I preferred spending time with my friends. |

| E | My parents have become my role models. |

| F | I want my children to have the same childhood as me. |

| G | I will never forget our family holidays. |

| H | It was hard for me to move away from my family. |

27 Speaker 1 .... [1]

28 Speaker 2 .... [1]

29 Speaker 3 .... [1]

30 Speaker 4 .... [1]

31 Speaker 5 .... [1]

32 Speaker 6 .... [1]

[Total: 6]

When you have finished doing this part of the test, go to the answer key for Section 2, Unit 2.2 and check your answers.

Your score: .... out of 6

Now think about your progress so far and answer the following questions:

- Was your score for Test 1, Exercise 4 higher than in Test 1, or not? Why do you think this is?

- After doing the **Reflection** section for this part of the exam, did you find it easier to do Test 2? What guidance did you find helpful?

- Is there anything that you still find difficult? What are you going to do to improve this?

Develop your skills

In Exercise 4, you listen to short monologues to test whether you can:

1   understand factual information (e.g. types of free time activities, ways of communicating)

2   understand more complex ideas (e.g. speakers' opinions, feelings, preferences, decisions)

3   understand how different ideas are connected (e.g. comparing the past and the present, changes in habits)

4   understand what speakers imply but do not say directly.

Try the following to improve these listening skills:

- After you have listened to this type of listening test, look at the audioscript. Try to find words and phrases that paraphrase the idea/opinion on the question paper. Also, look for examples of implied information in the script (e.g. *I only buy things when I absolutely have to* implies the speaker tries to avoid going shopping as much as they can).

- Watch/listen to debates on a range of topics/issues (e.g. advertising to children, small shops in city centres, road safety). Mute the beginning so that you do not hear the interviewer's question. Then listen to the rest and try to work out the topic/question from what the other speakers are saying. Then listen to the beginning and check. Also notice what phrases the speakers use to show they agree or disagree with the question/issue.

- Watch/listen to discussions and say whether the speakers agree with each other completely or partially. Listen to the same discussions again and note down the reasons the speakers give for their agreement or disagreement.

TIP

When you practise your listening using online resources, films, etc., only listen to short extracts (a similar length to the extracts used in the real exam). You can listen to a short extract more than once without getting tired and focus more easily on the language it uses.

TIP

Watching or listening to a range of audio recordings will also help you with your speaking test. You can learn some useful language and see how speakers develop their answers.

Test 1

 Exercise 5

You will hear an interview with Jessica Smith, who has just crossed the Pacific Ocean in a rowing boat with three other women. For each question, choose the correct answer, **A**, **B** or **C**, and put a tick (✓) in the appropriate box.

You will hear the interview twice.

Now look at Questions **33–40**.

33 What record did the women break?

  A the smallest number of crew members ☐

  B the fastest time to cross the Pacific ☐

  C the fewest stopovers made ☐

  [1]

34 The main reason why Jessica decided to take part in the crossing was…

  A to raise awareness of a charity ☐

  B to test her own abilities ☐

  C to make new friends. ☐

  [1]

35 What was most unusual about the boat?
   Jessica says that the most unusual thing about the boat was…

  A its size ☐

  B its colour ☐

  C its name. ☐

  [1]

36 Why did the crew have to learn to read each other's body language?

  A to avoid having arguments ☐

  B to build up trust with the others ☐

  C to spot the signs of extreme tiredness ☐

  [1]

37   Jessica would have loved to spend more time preparing for…

    A   the lack of sleep ☐

    B   the lack of space on the boat ☐

    C   the lack of contact with the outside world. ☐

    [1]

38   What was the most difficult aspect for the crew during the journey?

    A   boredom ☐

    B   physical injuries ☐

    C   unexpected changes ☐

    [1]

39   Why were the crew delayed at the end of their journey?

    A   One of the members became seriously ill. ☐

    B   The crew had very little energy left. ☐

    C   There was very bad weather. ☐

    [1]

40   What did Jessica look forward to doing first after they arrived?

    A   eating fresh food ☐

    B   having a shower ☐

    C   sleeping in a bed ☐

    [1]

    [Total: 8]

> When you have finished doing this part of the test, go to the answer key for Section 2, Unit 2.2 and check your answers.
>
> Your score: ………… out of 8

Reflection

Now think about the way you did Test 1, Exercise 5. Read the questions in the following table and put YES or NO to show you have, or have not, done these things. The questions remind you about the things you should do in Exercise 5 in the Listening exam. If some of your answers are NO, these are the areas you need to practise a bit more to improve your performance in the exam.

Before you started listening	YES or NO	Guidance
1 Did you read the eight questions carefully before listening?		In this exercise, read all eight questions before the audio recording starts. The audio recording is repeated at the end of the whole interview.
		The questions appear in the same order on the question paper as they do in the audio recording.
2 Did you highlight the important words in each question (**not** in options A–C) before listening?		Remember to highlight important words (e.g. *record*, *women*, *main reason*, *take part*). These will help you to select the correct idea from the audio recording and avoid the distractors.
3 Did you quickly scan the ideas in the options?		Do not worry about the options A–C too much at this stage. Mainly focus on the questions before you listen for the first time. The ideas in the audio recording will have different wording from the language used in the options on the question paper
While you were listening	**YES or NO**	**Guidance**
4 Did you take notes for each question?		It is difficult to read and listen at the same time. Try to follow these steps: 1 Focus on the highlighted words from each question. 2 Take notes of the idea that you think answers each question during the first listening. 3 Before you listen for the second time, quickly scan options A–C and circle the option that is the closest to the idea from your notes. 4 Check your answers when you listen to the interview for the second time.
5 Did you check your answers for each question during the second listening?		If you cannot decide between two options, put a question mark next to them. Decide which option is correct while you are listening for the second time.
After you finished listening	**YES or NO**	**Guidance**
6 Did you tick only one option for each question?		If you tick more than one box, you may **not** be given any marks for this question.
7 Did you make sure that you answered all the questions?		If you are still unsure which option is correct after the audio recording is played the second time, try to guess the answer.
8 Did you write your answers on the question paper only, at this stage?		You will be given **six minutes** at the end of the exam to transfer all your answers onto a **separate answer sheet**. You should not do it during the exam. You should use the time in between exercises to check your answers and read the questions in the next exercise.

If you answered 'No' to any of the questions in the **Reflection** section, try to follow all the guidance from this section when you do Test 2, Exercise 5.

Now do Test 2, Exercise 5.

Test 2

Exercise 5

You will hear an interview with a blogger called Darren Biggs, who travels around the world. For each question, choose the correct answer, **A**, **B** or **C**, and put a tick (✓) in the appropriate box.

You will hear the interview twice.

Now look at Questions **33–40**.

33   Why did Darren quit the job he had in the USA?

    A   He did not like the job routine. ☐

    B   He was not able to do his hobbies. ☐

    C   He was disappointed with his career. ☐

    [1]

34   How did Darren's family react to his decision?

    A   They were worried about his safety. ☐

    B   They tried to change his mind. ☐

    C   They thought he was joking. ☐

    [1]

35   Before leaving the USA, Darren had most trouble with…

    A   sorting out his documents ☐

    B   leaving his friends behind ☐

    C   selling his possessions. ☐

    [1]

36   How did Darren choose his first destination?

    A   He had been there before. ☐

    B   It was a sudden decision. ☐

    C   A friend had recommended it. ☐

    [1]

37   How does Darren earn extra money on his travels?

    A   He advertises sportswear. ☐

    B   He sells his photos. ☐

    C   He does seasonal jobs. ☐

    [1]

38 Why did Darren briefly return to the USA?

    A   He missed being with his friends and family.   ☐

    B   He needed to see a doctor after an injury.   ☐

    C   He wanted to check he had made the right choice.   ☐

                                        [1]

39 The most memorable moment for Darren so far has been…

    A   trekking in the jungle   ☐

    B   diving in the ocean   ☐

    C   meeting a local tribe.   ☐

                                        [1]

40 This experience has taught Darren to be…

    A   stronger   ☐

    B   open-minded   ☐

    C   determined.   ☐

                                        [1]

                                   [Total: 8]

> When you have finished doing this part of the test, go to the answer key for Section 2, Unit 2.2 and check your answers.
>
> Your score: .... out of 8

CHECK YOUR PROGRESS

Now think about your progress so far and answer the following questions:

- Was your score in Test 2, Exercise 5 higher than in Test 1, or not? Why do you think this is?

- After doing the **Reflection** section for this part of the exam, did you find it easier to do Test 2? What guidance did you find helpful?

- Is there anything that you still find difficult? What are you going to do to improve this?

Learn from mistakes

At the end of the Listening exam, you will be given six minutes to transfer your answers from the question paper onto a separate answer sheet.

a Download an example answer sheet from the digital resource. Use this answer sheet to copy your answers from Test 2. Use a timer to time yourself.

b Look at one student's answers on an example answer sheet. What did they do wrong in Questions 1–5?

Questions 1 to 8
1 A — B C — D
2 A — B ✗ C D
3 A B C ▬ D ▬
4 A (B) C D
5 A B C D
6 A B C ▬ D
7 A B ▬ C D
8 A B C D ▬

c Now check your answers on your answer sheet to make sure you did not make the same mistakes. If you did, remember not to make them again in the future.

Develop your skills

In Exercise 5, you listen to a semi-formal, or informal, interview to test whether you can:

1 understand factual information (e.g. types of activities, ways of communicating, sources of inspiration)

2 understand more complex ideas (e.g. speakers' experiences, opinions, feelings, preferences, decisions, future plans)

3 understand how different ideas are connected (e.g. comparing the past the present, changes in habits)

4 understand what speakers imply but do not say directly.

Try the following activities to help you improve these listening skills:

A After you have listened to this type of listening test, look at the audioscript. Highlight the words/phrases that express the idea in the correct option.

B Watch/listen to TV or radio interviews with various people (e.g. actors, scientists, singers, explorers).

- Before you listen, make two headings on a piece of paper – *Interviewee's answer/opinion* and *Extra information*.

- Listen to the interviewer's question and then the interviewee's answer. While you are listening to the answer, take notes under the correct heading to see what the main idea is and what the additional information is.

- Then listen to the answer again and write down the phrase that introduces the speaker's opinion (e.g. *As for me* and *I would say*) and other people's opinion (e.g. *According to …*, *In general*).

TIP

Use the answer sheet at the end of all the practice listening tests you do. This will help you get used to this for the real exam. You can also see if you can transfer all your answers in the given time. Remember not to rush when you are transferring your answers – you may make mistakes if you do.

TIP

Use a soft pencil to fill in the answer sheet. If you make a mistake, make sure you erase your first attempt completely.

Unit 2.3: Language focus

Look at Exercise 1, Question 1. Then listen to the audio recording and answer the question as you would in the real exam. Before you listen for the second time, read the guidance in the **Language focus** box and follow the instructions. Do the same for the remaining questions, 2–40.

> **TIP**
>
> To help you see which options you have already eliminated as wrong answers in each question, you can cross out the options/pictures (A, B, C or D) as you listen to the audio recording(s).

Test 3

 ### Exercise 1

You will hear eight short audio recordings. For each question, choose the correct answer, **A**, **B**, **C** or **D**, and put a tick (✓) in the appropriate box.

You will hear each audio recording twice.

1 What birthday presents does the woman decide to buy for her mother?

A ☐   B ☐   C ☐   D ☐   [1]

> **LANGUAGE FOCUS 1**
>
> The key words in the question are *woman* and *decide*. What are the woman's two final choices? Which phrases in the audio recording tell you that?

 2 What were most students unhappy about?

A ☐   B ☐   C ☐   D ☐   [1]

LANGUAGE FOCUS 2

The key words in the question are *most students* and *unhappy*. Which school facility is the correct answer? Which phrases in the audio recording tell you that?

  3 What does the man still need to buy before his trekking trip?

A    B    C    D

☐   ☐   ☐   ☐ [1]

LANGUAGE FOCUS 3

The key words in the question are *need to buy* and *before … trip*. Which option is the correct answer? Which phrases in the audio recording tell you that?

 4 Where do the friends agree to meet?

A    B    C    D

☐   ☐   ☐   ☐ [1]

LANGUAGE FOCUS 4

The key words in the question are *agree* and *meet*. Which place is the correct answer? Which phrases in the audio recording tell you that?

TIP

Some questions focus on **agreement**. To get the correct answer, you need to make sure that **both speakers** agree with the idea, not just one of them.

5 Which photograph did the couple like best at the exhibition?

A  **B**  **C**  **D**

☐ ☐ ☐ ☐ [1]

LANGUAGE FOCUS 5

The key words in the question are *the couple* and *like best*. Which photograph is the correct answer? Which phrases in the audio recording tell you that?

 6 Why did the boy have to stay at home last night?

A  **B** 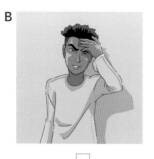 **C**  **D**

☐ ☐ ☐ ☐ [1]

LANGUAGE FOCUS 6

The key words in the question are *boy*, *stay at home* and *last night*. Which reason is the correct answer? Which phrases in the audio recording tell you that?

 7 Which course is the woman planning to do first at the local college?

A  **B**  **C**  **D**

☐ ☐ ☐ ☐ [1]

LANGUAGE FOCUS 7

The key words in the question are *woman*, *planning* and *first*. Which course is the correct answer? Which phrases in the audio recording tell you that?

 8 What did the local people raise money for at the recent charity event?

A  **B**  **C** 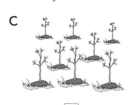 **D**

☐   ☐   ☐   ☐   [1]

[Total: 8]

LANGUAGE FOCUS 8

The key words in the question are *raise money for* and *recent ... event*. Which option is the correct answer? Which phrases in the audio recording tell you that?

When you have finished doing this part of the test, go to the answer key for Section 2, Unit 2.3 and check your answers.

Your score: .... out of 8

Language focus

Exercise A: Identifying distractors

You are going to focus on the vocabulary and grammar that helps you decide which details in the audio recording are distractors. Listen to the eight audio recordings again and find phrases that have the same, or very similar, meaning as the following phrases and definitions. Write your answers on the lines provided.

 1

I was planning to do something, but then I did not ....

Two phrases that tell you the mother does not/did not like something:

- ....

- ....

2

Most of you liked ....

Some of you did not like ....

It is OK for almost everybody ....

13 **3**

Three phrases that tell you the man does not want to, or does not need to, buy the item before his trip:

- ....
- ....
- ....

14 **4**

Two phrases that the boy uses to disagree with the girl:

- ....
- ....

15 **5**

I liked something more ....

I liked something less ....

16 **6**

My grandparents decided not to come to the family dinner ....

My grandparents did not want to drive in the rain ....

I am sure I got the headache because I studied hard in the morning ....

17 **7**

I did not think it would be worth the time I would spend doing it and the money I would pay for it ....

Two phrases that tell you that the woman was thinking about another option:

- ....
- ....

I want to do them after this one ....

18 **8**

We previously achieved good results ....

In the future, we would like to ....

CHECK YOUR PROGRESS

Now think about your progress so far and answer the following questions:

- Did you remember to use all the exam techniques you learnt in Unit 2.2?
- Was your score in Exercise 1 of this unit better or worse than your scores in Exercise 1 in Unit 2.2? Why do you think this is?
- After looking at the **Language focus** sections for this part of the exam, did you find it easier to answer the questions?
- Are you now better at recognising the correct detail and the distracting information?
- Is there anything that you still find difficult? What are you going to do to improve this?

Test 3

Exercise 2

You will hear five short audio recordings. For each question, choose the correct answer, **A**, **B** or **C**, and put a tick (✓) in the appropriate box.

You will hear each audio recording twice.

You will hear two students talking about the school trip they are on.

9 What did the girl forget to bring on the school trip?

    A   her sunglasses   ☐

    B   a phone charger   ☐

    C   suntan lotion   ☐

                                                  [1]

10 What do the students agree to do first?

    A   listen to a talk about dolphins   ☐

    B   go on a night walk   ☐

    C   try a surfing lesson   ☐

                                                  [1]

LANGUAGE FOCUS 9

The key words in the question are *forget to bring*. What did the girl forget to bring? Which two phrases in the audio recording tell you that?

LANGUAGE FOCUS 10

The key words in the question are *agree* and *first*. Do the students agree to do first what they find very exciting, or less exciting? Which phrase in the audio recording tells you what they want to do first? Which phrase in the audio recording tells you they both agree with this suggestion?

> **TIP**
>
> The words and phrases used in the options on the question paper are often different from the words and phrases used in the audio recording. However, they express the same, or a very similar, idea. This is called paraphrasing.

You will hear a man asking about a beach clean-up event he wants to join.

11 What information about the event was the man unable to find?

    A   the meeting point   ☐

    B   the finishing time   ☐

    C   the necessary equipment   ☐

                                                  [1]

12 What does the event organiser suggest the man should do next?

    A   do more research ☐

    B   phone back later ☐

    C   fill out an application form ☐

[1]

LANGUAGE FOCUS 11

The key words in the question are *information* and *unable to find*. Which information couldn't the man find? Which phrase in the audio recording tells you that?

LANGUAGE FOCUS 12

The key words in the question are *organiser*, *suggest* and *do next*. Which activity does the organiser suggest doing before anything else? Which phrase in the audio recording tells you that?

🎧 **You will hear a woman talking about her new dance class.**

13 The woman decided to join the dance class because of

    A   somebody's recommendation ☐

    B   her fitness level ☐

    C   a personal goal. ☐

[1]

14 What does the woman enjoy most about her dance class?

    A   the teaching style ☐

    B   the group dances ☐

    C   the timetable ☐

[1]

LANGUAGE FOCUS 13

The key words in the question are *decided to join* and *because of*. What is the woman's reason for joining? Which sentence in the audio recording tells you that?

LANGUAGE FOCUS 14

The key words in the question are *enjoy most* and *class*. Which activity does the woman enjoy a lot? Which sentence in the audio recording tells you that?

You will hear a man telling his friend about his recent holiday.

15 The man says that at the end of his holiday

    A he had to change his plans ☐

    B he regretted something ☐

    C he was surprised by someone. ☐

        [1]

16 Why was the man unable to do one of the guided walks?

    A He was not feeling very well. ☐

    B The weather was really bad. ☐

    C His alarm clock was not working. ☐

        [1]

LANGUAGE FOCUS 15

The key words in the question are *end* and *holiday*. Which option fully matches what the man says about the end of his holiday? Which phrase in the audio recording tells you that?

LANGUAGE FOCUS 16

The key words in the question are *why*, *unable to do* and *one of the … walks*. Which reason does the man give for *him* missing the guided walk? Which phrase in the audio recording tells you that?

You will hear a girl telling her mum about her first weeks at university.

17 How did the girl feel during her most recent lecture?

    A embarrassed about a mistake ☐

    B disappointed with the technology ☐

    C worried about the difficulty ☐

        [1]

18 What is the girl planning to do to earn some extra money?

  A   give private lessons ☐

  B   work in a supermarket ☐

  C   sell some of her possessions ☐

[1]

LANGUAGE FOCUS 17

The key words in the question are *feel* and *recent lecture*. Which feeling is linked to the most recent lecture? Which option fully matches what the girl says about her recent lecture? Which phrase/sentence in the audio recording tells you that?

LANGUAGE FOCUS 18

The key words in the question are *planning to do* and *earn … money*. Which way of earning some money does the girl prefer? Which sentence in the audio recording tells you that?

[Total: 10]

When you have finished doing this part of the test, go to the answer key for Section 2, Unit 2.3 and check your answers.

Your score: .... out of 10

Language focus

Exercise A: Identifying signals

In Exercise 2, each audio recording has answers to two questions. It is important to listen to the 'signals' that let you know that the speaker has started answering the second question. These 'signals' are normally words or phrases that paraphrase the second question, or signal a change in the topic of the conversation. Listen to the five audio recordings again and find the parts of the audio recording that act as the 'signals'. Write these words/phrases/sentences on the lines provided.

(19) **Questions 9 and 10** ....

(20) **Questions 11 and 12** ....

(21) **Questions 13 and 14** ....

(22) **Questions 15 and 16** ....

(23) **Questions 17 and 18** ....

> **TIP**
>
> The words and phrases used as 'signals', to let you know when the speaker in the audio recording has moved onto the next question, also appear in the talk in Exercises 3 and the interview in Exercise 5.

Exercise B: Paraphrasing

Now listen again to all five audio recordings. This time you are going to focus on the wording of options A–C in Questions 10–18 and how they are paraphrased in the audio recording. Listen to each audio recording and, when you hear a phrase, or sentence, that fully, or partially, paraphrases the idea in one of the options, write it on the line provided. The first option has been done for you as an example.

 10 A listen to a talk about dolphins – *presentation about dolphins* ....

    B go on a night walk ....

    C try a surfing lesson ....

 11 A the meeting point ....

    B the finishing time ....

    C the necessary equipment ....

    12 A do more research ....

    B phone back later ....

    C fill out an application form ....

 13 A somebody's recommendation ....

    B her fitness level ....

    C a personal goal ....

    14 A the teaching style ....

    B the group dances ....

    C the timetable ....

 15 A he had to change his plans ....

    B he regretted something ....

    C he was surprised by someone ....

    16 A he was not feeling very well ....

    B the weather was really bad ....

    C his alarm clock was not working ....

17 A embarrassed about a mistake ....

    B disappointed with the technology ....

    C worried about the difficulty ....

18 A giving private lessons ....

    B working in a supermarket ....

    C selling some of her possessions ....

Exercise C: Understanding feelings and opinions

You are going to focus on some more vocabulary and grammar that will help with your understanding for detail and a speaker's feelings and opinions. Listen to the five audio recordings again and find the phrases that have the same or very similar meaning to the following phrases. Write your answers on the lines provided.

19 **Questions 9 and 10**

That is right! ....

I think this is the most exciting one ....

I had the same idea as you ....

I am not as excited about this as about something else ....

Can't wait to do something / be really excited about something ....

20 **Questions 11 and 12**

There is no need to bring anything ....

It might be a good idea for you to do this ....

21 **Questions 13 and 14**

I have started (*used when talking about a new activity, like a hobby*) ....

I highly recommend this class ....

It is convenient for me ....

22 **Questions 15 and 16**

To get some free time on days when you normally work ....

The place was very busy ....

That surprised me ....

I discovered / I heard ....

It probably was not worth it ....

23 **Questions 17 and 18**

Difficult to understand ....

Initially, but not anymore ....

I am starting to feel OK about something that was challenging

at the start ....

Concerning something ....

Searching for / Trying to find ....

TIP

If you find doing any **Language focus** sections difficult, and cannot find the correct words and phrases by listening, you can read the relevant audioscript in the digital resource. However, try **not** to do this **too often** because it will not help you improve your listening skills.

CHECK YOUR PROGRESS

Now think about your progress so far and answer the following questions:

*   Did you remember to use all the exam techniques you learnt in Unit 2.2?

*   Was your score in Exercise 2 in this unit better or worse than your scores in Exercise 2 in Unit 2.2? Why do you think this is?

*   After looking at the **Language focus** sections for this part of the exam, was it easier for you to find the correct answers? Are you now better at recognising what the correct detail is and what the distracting information is?

*   Is there anything that you still find difficult? What are you going to do to improve this?

Test 3

Exercise 3

You will hear an expert in agriculture called Carlo Moretti giving a talk about underwater farming in Italy. For each question, choose the correct answer, **A**, **B** or **C**, and put a tick (✓) in the appropriate box.

You will hear the talk twice.

Now look at Questions **19–26.**

> **TIP**
>
> Remember: all three ideas, from options A–C, will be mentioned in the audio recording but only one is the correct answer and two are the distracting details.

Underwater farming

19 The idea of underwater farming was developed by … who also founded the project.

    A a marine scientist ☐

    B a scuba diver ☐

    C an ocean engineer ☐

    [1]

20 The project was given the name of …

    A Nemo's Garden ☐

    B Ocean Magic ☐

    C Ocean Reef Group. ☐

    [1]

21 The speaker compares the underwater structures to enormous …

    A rain drops ☐

    B balloons ☐

    C golf balls. ☐

    [1]

22 There were sometimes problems with … at the start of the project.

    A insects ☐

    B flooding ☐

    C plant disease ☐

    [1]

23 The red spectrum in light, which is necessary for plants to grow, can reach a maximum depth of … metres.

    A five ☐

    B eleven ☐

    C fifteen ☐

    [1]

24 The speaker was surprised that … can also be grown in underwater greenhouses.

    A strawberries ☐

    B wasabi ☐

    C beans ☐

    [1]

25 No … is required to grow plants under the sea.

  A fresh water ☐

  B power supply ☐

  C cooling system ☐

[1]

26 The speaker thinks that, in the future, … will benefit most from the project.

  A eco-tourism ☐

  B medical research ☐

  C fish farming ☐

[1]

[Total: 8]

Language focus

a After you have listened to the talk in Exercise 3 for the first time, look at the **Language focus** box following each question. These boxes contain guidance that will help you focus on the important vocabulary and grammar that you need to select the correct answer. Then listen to the audio recording again, and check your answers.

19 The idea of underwater farming was developed by a … who also founded the project.

  A a marine scientist

  B a scuba diver

  C an ocean engineer

[1]

> **TIP**
>
> Sometimes you hear exactly the same words as in options A–C on the question paper (e.g. options in Question 19). However, sometimes the ideas from options A–C may be paraphrased in the audio recording (e.g. options in Question 26).

LANGUAGE FOCUS 19

The key words in the sentence are *the idea* and *developed*. Focus on who was actually responsible for the development of this idea. Why are the other two jobs wrong?

20 The project was given the name of …

  A Nemo's Garden

  B Ocean Magic

  C Ocean Reef Group.

[1]

LANGUAGE FOCUS 20

The key words in the sentence are *project* and *name*. Focus on the actual name that the project was given. Why are the other two names wrong?

---

21 The speaker compares the underwater structures to enormous …

   A   rain drops

   B   balloons

   C   golf balls.

[1]

LANGUAGE FOCUS 21

The key words in the sentence are *the speaker*, *underwater structures* and *compares … to*. Focus on what the speaker thinks the structures look like, not what they actually are. Why are the other two options wrong?

---

22 There were sometimes problems with … at the start of the project.

   A   insects

   B   flooding

   C   plant disease

[1]

LANGUAGE FOCUS 22

The key words in the sentence are *problems*, *at the start* and *the project*. Focus on the problems connected with the underwater project. Why are the other two problems wrong?

---

23 The red spectrum in light, which is necessary for plants to grow, can reach a maximum depth of … metres.

   A   five

   B   eleven

   C   fifteen

[1]

LANGUAGE FOCUS 23

The key words in the sentence are *red spectrum* and *maximum depth*. Focus on the red spectrum in light and the depth it can reach. Why are the other two depths wrong?

24 The speaker was surprised that … can also be grown in underwater greenhouses.

   A   strawberries

   B   wasabi

   C   beans

[1]

LANGUAGE FOCUS 24

The key words in the sentence are *surprised* and *can also be grown*. Focus on something that Sergio has already grown in the underwater greenhouses, which surprised the speaker. Why are the other two options wrong?

25 No … is required to grow plants under the sea.

   A   fresh water

   B   power supply

   C   cooling system

[1]

LANGUAGE FOCUS 25

The key words are *no* and *required*. Focus on what Sergio does not need at all to grow his plants under the sea. Why are the other two options wrong?

26 The speaker thinks that, in the future, … will benefit most from the project.

   A   eco-tourism

   B   medical research

   C   fish farming

[1]

LANGUAGE FOCUS 26

The key words are *the speaker*, *future* and *benefit most*. Focus on which industry will benefit more than the other two. Why are the other two industries wrong?

[Total: 8]

When you have finished doing this part of the test, go to the answer key for Section 2, Unit 2.3 and check your answers.

Your score: .... out of 8

Language focus

b   You are going to focus on the vocabulary now. The following words and phrases are taken from Questions 19–26. Now listen again to the audio recording. Listen for the words and phrases that have the same or similar meaning. Write them on the lines provided.

19 the idea of ....

developed by ....

20 was given the name of ....

21 compare something to something else ....

enormous ....

22 at the start ....

there were problems ....

sometimes ....

23 is necessary for plants to grow ....

reach a depth of ....

maximum ....

24 was surprised ....

can also be grown ....

25 is required ....

no ....

26 benefit ....

most ....

CHECK YOUR PROGRESS

Now think about your progress so far and answer the following questions:

- Did you remember to use all the exam techniques you learnt in Unit 2.2?

- Was your score in Exercise 3 of this unit better or worse than your scores in Exercise 3 in Unit 2.2? Why do you think this is?

- After looking at the **Language focus** sections for this part of the exam, did you find it easier to answer the questions?

- Are you now better at recognising the correct detail and the distracting information?

- Is there anything that you still find difficult? What are you going to do to improve this?

Test 3

 Exercise 4

You will hear six people talking about keeping in touch with friends. For Questions **27–32**, choose from the list (**A–H**) which idea each speaker expresses. Write the correct letter (**A–H**) on the answer line. Use each letter only once. There are two extra letters that you do not need to use.

You will hear the audio recordings twice.

Now read statements **A–H**.

| A | I avoid contacting friends at certain times. |

| B | Calling my friends from abroad can be expensive. |

| C | I only text my closest friends from time to time. |

| D | I often go to social media sites to see what my friends are doing. |

| E | I feel nervous when I call friends I have not seen for a long time. |

| F | I should make more effort to call or write to friends when I am away. |

| G | Receiving photos from friends is better than reading emails. |

| H | I prefer to write letters to my friends. |

27 Speaker 1 .... [1]

28 Speaker 2 .... [1]

29 Speaker 3 .... [1]

30 Speaker 4 .... [1]

31 Speaker 5 .... [1]

32 Speaker 6 .... [1]

[Total: 6]

Language focus

a After you have listened to all six speakers for the first time, look at this **Language focus** section. For each speaker, there is a list of ideas, but only one idea is the correct answer, the remaining ideas are distractors. Listen to all six speakers again. To select the correct idea, make sure it fully matches what the speaker says. If it does not match exactly what the speaker says, it means it is a distractor. The following ideas are listed in the same order as they appear in the audio recording.

Speaker 1

B Calling my friends from abroad can be expensive.

H I prefer to write letters to my friends.

F I should make more effort to call or write to friends when I am away.

D I often go to social media sites to see what my friends are doing.

G Receiving photos from friends is better than reading emails.

Speaker 2

D I often go to social media sites to see what my friends are doing.

F I should make more effort to call or write to friends when I am away.

H I prefer to write letters to my friends.

E I feel nervous when I call friends I have not seen for a long time.

D I often go to social media sites to see what my friends are doing.

Speaker 3

G Receiving photos from friends is better than reading emails.

C I only text my closest friends from time to time.

A I avoid contacting friends at certain times.

F I should make more effort to call or write to friends when I am away.

B Calling my friends from abroad can be expensive.

Speaker 4

E   I feel nervous when I call friends I have not seen for a long time.

C   I only text my closest friends from time to time.

F   I should make more effort to call or write to friends when I am away.

D   I often go to social media sites to see what my friends are doing.

G   Receiving photos from friends is better than reading emails.

Speaker 5

A   I avoid contacting friends at certain times.

E   I feel nervous when I call friends I have not seen for a long time.

C   I only text my closest friends from time to time.

F   I should make more effort to call or write to friends when I am away.

Speaker 6

F   I should make more effort to call or write to friends when I am away.

H   I prefer to write letters to my friends.

C   I only text my closest friends from time to time.

D   I often go to social media sites to see what my friends are doing.

E   I feel nervous when I call friends I have not seen for a long time.

When you have finished doing this part of the test, go to the answer key for Section 2, Unit 2.3 and check your answers.

Your score: .... out of 6

b   Now you are going to focus on the vocabulary. The following words and phrases are taken from statements **A–H** on the question paper. Listen again to the six speakers and find the words/phrases with the same or very similar meaning. Write your answers on the lines provided.

TIP

Remember – in Exercise 4, most of the ideas and opinions in the audio recording will be *implied*. This means that the language used in the audio recording may only suggest the idea from the question paper without saying it directly.

Speaker 1

calling ....

friends ....

abroad ....

expensive ....

Speaker 2

write ....

I prefer ....

Speaker 3

receiving ....

photos ....

is better ....

Speaker 4

social media sites ....

see ....

what my friends are doing ....

Speaker 5

only ....

text from time to time ....

Speaker 6

I feel nervous ....

call ....

I have not seen for a long time ....

CHECK YOUR PROGRESS

Now think about your progress so far and answer the following questions:

- Did you remember to use all the exam techniques you learnt in Unit 2.2?

- Was your score in Exercise 4 of this unit better or worse than your scores in Exercise 4 in Unit 2.2? Why do you think this is?

- After looking at the **Language focus** sections for this part of the exam, did you find it easier to answer the questions?

- Are you now better at recognising the correct detail and the distracting information?

- Is there anything that you still find difficult? What are you going to do to improve this?

Test 3

Exercise 5

You will hear an interview with a businesswoman called Fatima Karimi, who started an online language school. For each question, choose the correct answer, **A**, **B** or **C**, and put a tick (✓) in the appropriate box.

You will hear the interview twice.

Now look at Questions **33–40**.

33 Why did Fatima learn languages when she was little?

    A   Her mother made her. ☐

    B   She dreamed of travelling. ☐

    C   The family moved around a lot. ☐

    [1]

> **TIP**
>
> Listen carefully to the interviewer's questions. They are similar to the questions on the question paper and will guide you through the interview.

34 Just before starting her online language school, Fatima was

    A   unemployed ☐

    B   studying at university ☐

    C   working for a successful company. ☐

    [1]

35 What inspired Fatima to offer online language courses?

    A   Her relative did not complete a course because of the timetable. ☐

    B   Her relative had a bad experience with other students. ☐

    C   Her relative could not find the right teacher. ☐

    [1]

36 How does Fatima prefer to choose her future employees?

    A   She reads their application letters. ☐

    B   She receives a personal recommendation. ☐

    C   She has a face-to-face interview with them. ☐

    [1]

37 Most of Fatima's customers say they like her online language courses because

    A   they can study wherever and whenever they want ☐

    B   it feels like more than just learning a language ☐

    C   the lessons are similar to an online conversation. ☐

    [1]

38 Why did Fatima take a course using her own online language school?

    A   She wanted to test the system. ☐

    B   She wanted to learn a new language. ☐

    C   She wanted to check the teaching quality. ☐

    [1]

39 What is the biggest benefit of the online language school for Fatima?

    A   She can often travel abroad. ☐

    B   She has become more confident. ☐

    C   She works with an international team. ☐

    [1]

40 What is Fatima planning to do next?

    A   She hopes to expand the range of courses she provides. ☐

    B   She wants to focus more on language courses for companies. ☐

    C   She aims to make her online language school known worldwide. ☐

    [1]

    [Total: 8]

Language focus

a   After you have listened to the interview in Exercise 5 for the first time, look at the **Language focus** box following each question. These boxes contain guidance that will help you focus on the important vocabulary and grammar that you need to select the correct answer. Then listen to the audio recording again, and check your answers.

33 Why did Fatima learn languages when she was little?

    A   Her mother made her. ☐

    B   She dreamed of travelling. ☐

    C   The family moved around a lot. ☐

    [1]

> **LANGUAGE FOCUS 33**
>
> The key words in the question are *why*, *learn languages* and *little*. What was Fatima's reason for learning languages when she was little? Which phrase in the audio recording tells you that? Why are the other two options wrong?

34   Just before starting her online language school, Fatima was

    A   unemployed ☐

    B   studying at university ☐

    C   working for a successful company. ☐

    [1]

LANGUAGE FOCUS 34

The key words in the question are *just before*, *starting* and *her ... school*. What happened last before she started her new business? Which two sentences in the audio recording tell you that? Why are the other two options wrong?

---

35   What inspired Fatima to offer online language courses?

    A   Her relative did not complete a course because of the timetable. ☐

    B   Her relative had a bad experience with other students. ☐

    C   Her relative could not find the right teacher. ☐

    [1]

LANGUAGE FOCUS 35

The key words in the question are *what inspired* and *Fatima*. Focus on what inspired her, not what other people say. Which phrase in the audio recording tells you that? Why are the other two options wrong?

---

36   How does Fatima prefer to choose her future employees?

    A   She reads their application letters. ☐

    B   She receives a personal recommendation. ☐

    C   She has a face-to-face interview with them. ☐

    [1]

LANGUAGE FOCUS 36

The key words in the question are *how*, *prefer* and *choose ... employees*. What is Fatima's favourite way of choosing her employees? Which sentence in the audio recording tells you that? Why are the other two options wrong?

37 Most of Fatima's customers say they like her online language courses because

    A   they can study wherever and whenever they want   ☐

    B   it feels like more than just learning a language   ☐

    C   the lessons are similar to an online conversation.   ☐

                                                                           [1]

LANGUAGE FOCUS 37

The key words in the question are *most*, *like* and *because*. What is the reason why most students like the online courses? Which sentence in the audio recording tells you that? Why are the other two options wrong?

38 Why did Fatima take a course using her own online language school?

    A   She wanted to test the system.   ☐

    B   She wanted to learn a new language.   ☐

    C   She wanted to check the teaching quality.   ☐

                                                                           [1]

LANGUAGE FOCUS 38

The key words in the question are *why*, *Fatima* and *take a course*. What was the real reason behind Fatima's decision to use her own language school to do a course? Which sentence in the audio recording tells you that? Why are the other two options wrong?

39 What is the biggest benefit of the online language school for Fatima?

    A   She can often travel abroad.   ☐

    B   She has become more confident.   ☐

    C   She works with an international team.   ☐

                                                                           [1]

LANGUAGE FOCUS 39

The key words in the question are *biggest benefit* and *for Fatima*. Fatima mentions more benefits, but which one is the most important for her? Which phrase in the audio recording tells you that? Why are the other two options wrong?

40 What is Fatima planning to do next?

    A   She hopes to expand the range of courses she provides. ☐

    B   She wants to focus more on language courses for companies. ☐

    C   She aims to make her online language school known worldwide. ☐

[1]

LANGUAGE FOCUS 40

The key words in the question are *planning* and *next*. Which idea is about Fatima's future plan? Which sentence in the audio recording tells you that? Also, focus on the tenses Fatima uses in the audio recording and what the tenses tell us? Why are the other two options wrong?

When you have finished doing this part of the test, go to the answer key for Section 2, Unit 2.3 and check your answers.

Your score: .... out of 8

Language focus

b You are going to focus on some more vocabulary and grammar that will help with your understanding of detail and a speaker's feelings and opinions. Listen to the interview again and find the phrases that have the same or very similar meaning to the following phrases. Write your answers on the lines provided.

33 I could speak … very well ....

    In addition to something ....

    I managed to learn something very well / I became very good at

    something ....

    I had no other choice / I had to do this ....

34 As a child ....

    I did not really think / It did not cross my mind ....

    I found myself in a particular situation ....

    Very boring ....

35 Did not have a good relationship with ....

    Left a course before it officially finished ....

36 I have to do something else first ....

    To consider something ....

TIP

When you check the meaning of new vocabulary, try to use a **monolingual English dictionary** for learners. This is a dictionary that uses English to explain the meaning and it will show you how to use the word/phrase in a sentence. This type of dictionary will also improve your speaking fluency as you will not be translating in your head before you say it.

37 Was the most important thing for me ....

Starting a new company ....

They really like that ....

38 In addition to my main intention, it was also convenient that I wanted to

improve ....

It was the logical thing to do ....

This was not what I had planned to do ....

39 It is definitely / I must admit ....

40 We are very happy because we have been able to realise our

ambition ....

CHECK YOUR PROGRESS

Now think about your progress so far and answer the following questions:

- Did you remember to use all the exam techniques you learnt in Unit 2.2?
- Was your score in Exercise 5 of this unit better or worse than your scores in Exercise 5 in Unit 2.2? Why do you think this is?
- After looking at the **Language focus** sections for this part of the exam, did you find it easier to answer the questions?
- Are you now better at recognising the correct detail and the distracting information?
- Is there anything that you still find difficult? What are you going to do to improve this?

Now go to Unit 2.4 and try to do Test 4 under exam conditions to see how well you do. Remember to:

- use all the exam techniques you learned in Unit 2.2
- focus on the language that leads you to the correct answer
- avoid the distracting information which is wrong.

Good luck!

Unit 2.4: Test yourself

Test 4

Exercise 1

You will hear eight short audio recordings. For each question, choose the correct answer, **A**, **B**, **C** or **D**, and put a tick (✓) in the appropriate box.
You will hear each audio recording twice.

1   What time does the mother expect to be back from work today?

A 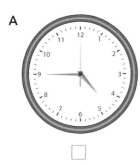   B 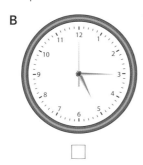   C 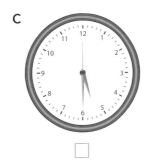   D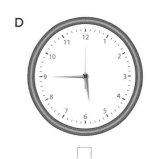

☐   ☐   ☐   ☐   [1]

2   What film are the friends going to see tonight?

A    B    C    D

☐   ☐   ☐   ☐   [1]

3   What birthday presents did the girl buy for her sister?

A    B

☐   ☐

C    D

☐   ☐   [1]

4   Who are the boy's new neighbours?

A    B 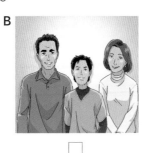   C 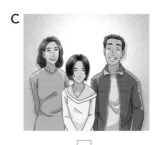   D

☐ ☐ ☐ ☐ [1]

5   Where did the man leave his phone?

A    B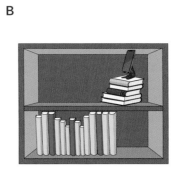

☐ ☐

C 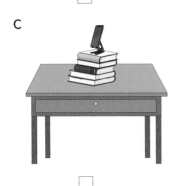   D

☐ ☐ [1]

6   Which activity did the girl enjoy most at the summer camp?

A    B    C    D

☐ ☐ ☐ ☐ [1]

7   What did the woman dislike most about the hotel she stayed at?

A   B   C   D

☐   ☐   ☐   ☐   [1]

8   Why is the boy late for his football practice?

A   B   C   D

☐   ☐   ☐   ☐   [1]

[Total: 8]

When you have finished doing this part of the test, go to the answer key for Section 2, Unit 2.4 and check your answers.

Your score: .... out of 8

Exercise 2

You will hear five short audio recordings. For each question, choose the correct answer, **A**, **B** or **C**, and put a tick (✓) in the appropriate box.

You will hear each audio recording twice.

You will hear a teacher telling students about their next school trip.

9   What do the students have to take with them?

A   enough food   ☐

B   suitable clothes   ☐

C   something to drink   ☐

[1]

10 After the school trip, the teacher wants the students to give a presentation about

    A environmental effects ☐

    B job satisfaction ☐

    C food production. ☐

    [1]

You will hear a boy telling his friend about a water sport he has taken up recently.

11 How did the boy first find out about underwater hockey?

    A A relative told him about it. ☐

    B A local sports centre advertised it. ☐

    C He saw a TV documentary about it. ☐

    [1]

12 Which skill is the boy finding difficult to improve?

    A moving fast underwater ☐

    B holding his breath ☐

    C swimming ☐

    [1]

You will hear a girl leaving a phone message for her friend about her adventure holiday.

13 What is the girl looking forward to on her holiday?

    A meeting new people ☐

    B spending time in the countryside ☐

    C learning about the local wildlife ☐

    [1]

14 The girl needs to borrow her friend's backpack because hers is

    A damaged ☐

    B too small ☐

    C missing. ☐

    [1]

You will hear two friends talking about a tennis match they went to.

15 What were the friends most disappointed about?

    A   the facilities for the spectators ☐

    B   the weather on the day ☐

    C   the public transport to get there ☐

       [1]

16 The friends agree that their favourite player lost because of

    A   his recent injury ☐

    B   his lack of experience ☐

    C   his attitude during the game. ☐

       [1]

You will hear a part of an interview with someone who works as a night sky officer.

17 What is the woman's favourite part of the job?

    A   the silence and darkness ☐

    B   raising awareness ☐

    C   the remote location ☐

       [1]

18 How did the woman's friends react to her job?

    A   They were curious. ☐

    B   They were surprised. ☐

    C   They were worried. ☐

       [1]

> When you have finished doing this part of the test, go to the answer key for Section 2, Unit 2.4 and check your answers.
>
> Your score: .... out of 8

Exercise 3

You will hear a clothes designer called Lee Chan giving a talk about the invention of waterproof fabric and the Macintosh raincoat. For each question, choose the correct answer, **A**, **B** or **C**, and put a tick (✓) in the appropriate box.

You will hear the talk twice.

The invention of waterproof material and the Macintosh raincoat

19 Charles Macintosh was first employed as a …

   A chemist ☐

   B clerk ☐

   C tailor. ☐

    [1]

20 Macintosh used a mixture containing … to waterproof clothing material.

   A rubber ☐

   B wax ☐

   C oil ☐

    [1]

21 Early waterproof material became … in warmer weather.

   A smelly ☐

   B stiff ☐

   C sticky ☐

    [1]

22 The speaker claims that it was hard for Macintosh to find people who would … his waterproof material.

   A produce ☐

   B sew ☐

   C wear ☐

    [1]

23 The first Macintosh coat was sold in …

   A 1818 ☐

   B 1823 ☐

   C 1824. ☐

    [1]

24 The speaker was surprised to learn that waterproof clothing was also supplied to ...

   A police officers ☐

   B polar explorers ☐

   C railway workers. ☐

       [1]

25 Recently, the Macintosh raincoat has become increasingly popular in ...

   A Japan ☐

   B France ☐

   C America. ☐

       [1]

26 What many people do not realise about the production of the Macintosh raincoat is that ...

   A the techniques are still the same ☐

   B some parts of the coat are glued ☐

   C the material is now made abroad. ☐

       [1]

       [Total: 8]

> When you have finished doing this part of the test, go to the answer key for Section 2, Unit 2.4 and check your answers.
>
> Your score: .... out of 8

Exercise 4

You will hear six people talking about their holidays. For Questions 27–32, choose from the list (**A–H**) which idea each speaker expresses. Write the letter (**A–H**) on the answer line. Use each letter only once. There are two extra letters that you do not need to use.

You will hear the audio recording twice.

Now read statements **A–H**.

A	I regret paying so much money for the holiday.

B	I found the locals very friendly.

C	I thought the quality of the accommodation was poor.

D	I worried about something unnecessarily.

E	I learnt a new skill while I was there.

F	I have decided to go back there again.

G	I was disappointed by the weather.

H	I should not have gone on my own.

27 Speaker 1 ....   [1]

28 Speaker 2 ....   [1]

29 Speaker 3 ....   [1]

30 Speaker 4 ....   [1]

31 Speaker 5 ....   [1]

32 Speaker 6 ....   [1]

[Total: 6]

When you have finished doing this part of the test, go to the answer key for Section 2, Unit 2.4 and check your answers.

Your score: .... out of 6

Exercise 5

You will hear an interview with Michael Vitko, a young adventurer, who has travelled to the Arctic Circle on his motorbike. Listen to the interview and look at the questions. For each question, choose the correct answer, **A**, **B** or **C**, and put a tick (✔) in the appropriate box.

You will hear the interview twice.

Now look at Questions 33–40.

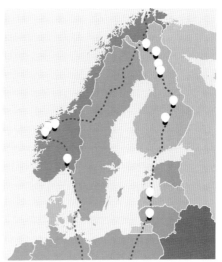

33 What gave Michael the idea to ride a motorbike to the Arctic Circle?

    A   a documentary he watched about a similar trip   ☐

    B   a conversation he had with a friend   ☐

    C   a book he read as a small child   ☐

    [1]

34 Michael says that the most important part of the preparation for the journey was

    A   planning the route very carefully   ☐

    B   checking the motorbike was working   ☐

    C   making sure he had enough money.   ☐

    [1]

35 Why did another motorcyclist join Michael in Lithuania?

    A   Michael was feeling lonely.   ☐

    B   Michael wanted someone to film him.   ☐

    C   They were both going in the same direction.   ☐

    [1]

36 Michael did not worry when his motorbike broke down because ...

    A he had prepared an alternative route ☐

    B he was able to obtain spare parts ☐

    C he had somewhere to stay. ☐

                                                       [1]

37 What did Michael find most challenging on his journey?

    A the extreme weather ☐

    B the communication ☐

    C the ferry crossings ☐

                                                       [1]

38 What made the biggest impression on Michael during his journey?

    A the silence he experienced in the wild ☐

    B the varied landscape he witnessed ☐

    C the kindness of the people he met ☐

                                                       [1]

39 How did Michael feel as soon as he returned home?

    A exhausted ☐

    B confused ☐

    C disappointed ☐

                                                       [1]

40 Michael says that riding his Jawa motorbike has ...

    A allowed him to have new experiences ☐

    B given him ideas about what to do next ☐

    C taught him to be more responsible. ☐

                                                       [1]

                                                      [Total: 8]

> When you have finished doing this part of the test, go to the answer key for Section 2, Unit 2.4 and check your answers.
>
> Your score: .... out of 8

Unit 3.1: About the exam

How much do you already know about the Speaking exam? Can you answer the following questions?

1 How many parts are there in the Speaking exam? .... [1]

2 How many students are examined at the same time? .... [1]

3 How many examiners are present during the exam? .... [1]

4 Look at the following table. Can you match each part of the exam with the

correct description (**A–E**)? .... [5]

Speaking exam*		
Introduction (up to 1 minute)	A	The examiner asks the student three questions about a topic. These questions are on the same everyday topic (e.g. travelling, the local area, music, friendship). Students receive marks for this part of the test.
Warm-up (1–2 minutes)	B	The examiner welcomes the student, states the student's name and number. Then the examiner gives the student a brief explanation of what is going to happen during the Speaking exam.
Part 1: Interview (2–3 minutes)	C	The examiner asks the student up to four questions. These are all opinion based and further develop the ideas from the previous part.
Part 2: Short talk (3–4 minutes)	D	The examiner asks the student a few questions about themselves (e.g. hobbies, the weekend, school life, future plans). This gives the student a chance to get used to talking to the examiner and relax before the assessed parts of the exam start.
Part 3: Discussion (3–4 minutes)	E	The examiner gives the student a topic card (e.g. choosing a new hobby, planning a trip). The student is asked to discuss, for example, the advantages and disadvantages of two options, compare and contrast two ideas. The student has one minute preparation time to think about their answers. Students are not allowed to write anything down. Then the student talks on their own for approximately two minutes. At the end, the student should say which idea they would prefer and explain why. The examiner then takes back the topic card.

* The whole Speaking exam is recorded.

5 Are all parts of the Speaking exam assessed? .... [1]

6 Can you see the questions that the examiner asks you in all parts of

the exam? .... [1]

7 What is the total number of marks you can get? .... [1]

8 How long does the whole Speaking exam last? .... [1]

9 Can you use a dictionary during the exam? .... [1]

10 Are you allowed to write down any notes? .... [1]

11 Are you allowed to speak in your first language with the examiner during

the exam? .... [1]

12 Are you allowed to ask for clarification in English if you don't understand

a question? .... [1]

13 Are you told whether you have passed at the end of the exam? .... [1]

[Total: 17]

> Now watch the complete Speaking exam (Video 1) and check your answers. If you are still unsure about the answers after you have watched the video, go to the answer key for Section 3, Unit 3.1. How many answers did you get right?
>
> Your score:...................... out of 17

01

CHECK YOUR PROGRESS

Was there anything you didn't know about the Speaking exam? Now test yourself to see if you can remember everything mentioned in the previous exercise. Are the following statements true (T) or false (F)? Circle the correct letter for each statement. If the statement is false, say what the correct answer is.

1	If there are a lot of students, sometimes two students can take the Speaking exam in pairs.	T / F
2	The examiner tells the student what the exam involves at the start of the exam.	T / F
3	The student is also given a piece of paper in case they want to write down some notes.	T / F
4	The questions the examiner asks in the warm-up are about the student's everyday life.	T / F
5	At the end of the warm-up, the student can choose the topic cards that they would like to talk about in the exam.	T / F
6	In Part 1, the interview, the student is asked two questions.	T / F
7	In Part 2, the short talk, the student is given a topic card with the question on it and can keep the card until the end of the short talk.	T / F
8	In Part 2, the short talk, the student has to start talking straight after the examiner hands over the topic card.	T / F
9	In Part 2, the short talk, the student can choose to talk about one of the two options only.	T / F
10	In Part 3, the discussion, the examiner asks questions that include everyday topics as well as opinion-based questions.	T / F
11	In Part 3, the discussion, the student is always asked four questions.	T / F
12	In Part 3, the discussion, the examiner asks questions about a topic that is similar to the topic in Part 2.	T / F
13	Students always have to agree with the ideas in the questions.	T / F
14	At the end of the exam, the examiner will tell the student whether they have passed or not.	T / F
15	Students are given marks for their performance in all parts of the exam, including the warm-up.	T / F
16	Only the assessed parts of the exam are recorded by the examiner.	T / F
17	Students can use a dictionary or ask the examiner how to say some words in English.	T / F
18	It is OK to give short answers, for example, yes/no answers.	T / F
19	If the examiner asks extra questions, this means that the student is not doing well in the exam.	T / F
20	If students do not know what else to say, they can talk about whatever topic they want.	T / F
21	There is a time limit to each part of the Speaking exam and the examiner will stop the student when this time limit is reached.	T / F

Now go to the answer key for Section 3, Unit 3.1 and check your answers.

Your score:..................... out of 21

Unit 3.2: Exam strategies

What are the examiners looking for?

In the Speaking exam you are marked on:

- grammar
- vocabulary
- development
- pronunciation.

a   The following list shows features that the examiners will be looking for in your speaking. Look at the list and decide whether the features are connected with grammar, vocabulary, development or pronunciation. Then complete the following table by putting the features under the correct heading.

Features

- maintaining communication
- precise use of words and phrases
- intonation
- the ability to express opinions on a range of issues
- complex sentences with linking words/phrases
- a range of words and phrases
- a range of grammatical structures
- how well developed the ideas are
- speaking clearly
- grammatical accuracy
- the ability to talk about a range of ideas
- how relevant the answers are.

Grammar	Vocabulary	Development	Pronunciation
•	•	•	•
•	•	•	•
•	•	•	
	•		

b Look at the descriptions **A–F**. They tell you how well you can do things when you speak. Can you put them next to the correct marks in the following table?

A These marks are given to students who:

- use a very small range of simple grammatical structures with frequent errors, which often make the meaning unclear
- use a very small range of vocabulary to express very simple opinions and talk about very simple ideas
- find it difficult to discuss things, despite a lot of support, and rarely develop their ideas, which are sometimes irrelevant
- have a lot of pronunciation and intonation issues and are often unclear.

B These marks are given to students who:

- do not give any answers.

C These marks are given to students who:

- use a range of complex and simple grammatical structures with no, or very few, errors
- use a wide range of vocabulary to express opinions and talk about different ideas with some precision
- discuss things without support and give relevant and well-developed answers
- always have clear pronunciation and use rising and falling intonation.

D   These marks are given to students who:

- only use some words, or very short phrases, instead of grammatical structures and the meaning is always unclear

- only use a few words and find it difficult to express opinions or talk about any topic

- cannot discuss things despite a lot of support and only occasionally give single words as their answers

- have serious pronunciation and intonation issues and cannot be understood.

E   These marks are given to students who:

- use a range of simple grammatical structures with no, or very few, errors

- try to use some complex grammatical structures, but not always correctly

- use a good range of vocabulary correctly to express opinions and talk about different ideas

- discuss things with occasional support and give relevant and, mostly, developed answers

- have a few pronunciation issues, but sound clear and sometimes use rising and falling intonation.

F   These marks are given to students who:

- use a range of simple grammatical structures, but with some errors that sometimes make the meaning unclear

- rarely try to use any complex grammatical structures

- use a range of vocabulary, mostly correctly, to express simple opinions and talk about simple ideas

- discuss things with frequent support and give relevant and sometimes developed ideas

- have pronunciation issues, but mostly sound clear and rarely use rising and falling intonation.

Marks	Description
9–10	
7–8	
5–6	
3–4	
1–2	
0	

TIP

After you complete the table with the descriptions, use it as a simplified mark scheme to assess your own speaking OR use the complete mark scheme from the **Assessment criteria** section at the start of the book.

First, do the exercise in Test 1 as you would in the real exam. Then look at the **Reflection** section to see some guidance on how to do this type of exercise. Also, look at the **Learn from mistakes** section to see common mistakes made by other students. Finally, do the same type of exercise in Test 2 to see if you have improved.

Test 1

Part 1: Interview

a Look at the speaking card **Music**. Give your answers to the questions in all three bullet points. You should talk for 2–3 minutes.

TIP

When you practise giving your answers to the questions on the speaking card, you can ask someone to act as the examiner to read out the questions to you. You should also use a timer to see if you can talk for the required length of time.

SPEAKING CARD

Music

- What music do you enjoy listening to, and why?

- Can you tell me about occasions when people usually listen to music?

- Do you think people's taste in music changes with age?

---

b When you have finished giving your answers to all three questions on the speaking card **Music**, look at the simplified mark scheme in the **What are the examiners looking for?** section. What marks do you think you would get for your speaking?

Your score for grammar:...................... out of 10

Your score for vocabulary:...................... out of 10

Your score for development:...................... out of 10

Your score for pronunciation:...................... out of 10

[Total: 40]

TIP

It is a good idea to record yourself when you are practising answering exam questions. When you watch your performance again, you can see better what you did well and what you need to improve.

Reflection

Now think about the way you did Test 1, Part 1 (speaking card **Music**). Read the questions in the following table and put YES or NO to show you have, or have not, done these things. The questions remind you about the things you should do in Part 1 of the Speaking exam. If some of your answers are NO, these are the areas you need to practise a bit more to improve your performance in the exam.

During the interview (Part 1)	YES or NO	Guidance
1 Did you speak for 2–3 minutes?		
2 Did you give answers to all three questions in the order they are given on the card?		

During the interview (Part 1)	YES or NO	Guidance
3 Did you answer everything each question asked for (e.g. give a reason why)?		Listen carefully to the questions to make sure you answer the whole question. Remember, if you do not understand any words from the question, you can ask the examiner for clarification.
4 Did you give answers that were well developed (e.g. by providing examples)?		To develop your answers, you can compare the present and the past, give an example of a personal experience, compare what you do with what other people do, make predictions of what might happen in the future, etc. But even these extra details need to be on the same topic as the question.
5 Did you talk fluently, without pausing for too long?		Remember, short pauses are a natural part of speaking and are OK. It is very long silences that you should try and avoid.
6 Did you link your ideas using appropriate phrases (e.g. *what is more, on the other hand*)?		
7 Did you use a range of grammatical structures (e.g. different tenses)?		
8 Did you use a wide range of vocabulary?		
9 Did you sound clear?		Remember, pronunciation is **not** about what accents people have, but how clear they sound.
10 Did you use rising and falling intonation in your answers?		It is also important to use rising and falling intonation, and to pause now and again, so that you do not sound monotonous or bored.

Learn from mistakes

a Now watch Video 2. In this recording, one student is giving his answers to the questions from the speaking card **Music**. Does the student give similar answers to yours?

b Look at the simplified mark scheme in the **What are the examiners looking for?** section. Answer the following questions and complete the student's mark card.

- What marks would the student get?

- What does the student do well?

- What does the student need to improve?

TIP

In the real exam, you will only receive one set of marks for your performance in the whole exam.

Student A: Peter

Grammar: ....

Vocabulary: ....

Development: ....

Pronunciation: ....

Total mark: ....

Strengths: ....

....

Weaknesses: ....

....

c   Most students find it difficult to develop the ideas in their answers. Now look at some sample answers given by students to the speaking card **Music**. The answers are very short. First, think of ways that you could develop them. Then compare your ideas with the suggestions. Now imagine you are the student and give the answers again, but this time make sure they are well developed.

> I love pop music because I love dancing to it.

To develop this answer, you can:

- compare your interest in music with your other friends

- contrast what music relaxes you and what music makes you bored/annoyed, and say why.

> People listen to music when they are commuting to work.

To develop this answer, you can talk about:

- yourself and other people you know (e.g. friends, parents, older people)

- different times of day

- celebrations (e.g. weddings, parties, religious events).

> My father told me he used to listen to rock music. Now he only listens to more serious music like jazz.

To develop this answer, you can:

- contrast your interest in music with your grandparents' or your younger siblings'

- explain the reasons why different generations listen to music

- try to predict what music you might listen to in the future.

d Now watch Video 2 again. After Peter gives his answers, pause the recording and develop his answers with extra ideas of your own.

Now you are ready to do Test 2, Part 1 (speaking card **Television**). Remember to use everything you have learnt so far when you give your answers.

Test 2

Part 1: Interview

a Look at the speaking card **Television**. Give your answers to the questions in all three bullet points. You should talk for 2–3 minutes.

SPEAKING CARD

Television

- What TV programmes are popular in your country, and why?

- Can you tell me about a time when you watched something on TV with someone else and what happened while you were watching?

- What do you think the advantages and disadvantages of children watching TV are?

When you have finished giving your answers to all the prompts on the speaking card **Television**, look at the simplified mark scheme in the **What are the examiners looking for?** section. What marks do you think you would get for your speaking?

Your score for grammar:...................... out of 10

Your score for vocabulary:...................... out of 10

Your score for development:...................... out of 10

Your score for pronunciation:...................... out of 10

[Total: 40]

Now think about your progress so far and answer the following questions:

- Was your score in Test 2 higher than in Test 1, or not? Why do you think this is?

- After doing the **Reflection** section, did you find it easier to do Test 2? What guidance did you find helpful?

- Is there anything you still find difficult? What are you going to do to improve this?

Test 1

Part 2: Short talk

a   Look at the speaking card **A new hobby**. Read the card very carefully and then spend one minute thinking about your answers. After one minute, start giving your short talk. You should talk for two minutes.

SPEAKING CARD

A new hobby

You have decided to take up a new hobby. You are considering the following options:

- cooking

- playing volleyball.

Compare the two options and say which one you would prefer, and why.

TIP

This is the only part of the test when you will be given the speaking card to look at. In the other parts of the test, the examiner will only read out the questions to you.

b   When you have finished giving your short talk on the speaking card **A new hobby**, look at the simplified mark scheme in the **What are the examiners looking for?** section. What marks do you think you would get for your speaking?

Your score for grammar:...................... out of 10

Your score for vocabulary:...................... out of 10

Your score for development:...................... out of 10

Your score for pronunciation:...................... out of 10

[Total: 40]

Reflection

Now think about the way you did Test 1, Part 2 (speaking card **A new hobby**). Read the questions in the following table and put YES or NO to show you have, or have not, done these things. The following questions remind you about the things you should do in Part 2 of the Speaking exam. If some of your answers are NO, these are the areas you need to practise a bit more to improve your performance in the exam.

Before the short talk (Part 2)	YES or NO	Guidance
1 Did you spend one minute preparing your answers?		You are not allowed to write any notes down. That is why it is very important to plan a few ideas for each bullet point in your head before you start speaking.

During the short talk (Part 2)	YES or NO	Guidance
2 Did you make sure your short talk was two minutes long?		It is a good idea to time yourself when you are preparing for the exam to get used to the time limit of two minutes. In the real exam, the examiner will ask you if you want to say anything else if you finish too early. If you go over two minutes, the examiner will stop you.
3 Did you say something about both options in the bullet points?		If you only talk about one of the options, you may lose marks for the development of ideas.
4 Did you compare the two options?		In this part of the exam, you may be asked to: compare two ideas, talk about the advantages and disadvantages or how easy or difficult something is.
5 Did you say which option you would prefer and explain why?		You should talk about your personal preference and give reasons for it at the end of your short talk.
6 Did you give answers that were well developed (e.g. giving reasons or explanations)?		
7 Did you link your ideas using appropriate phrases (e.g. *in addition to, however*)?		When you give a short talk, it is important to use linking words and rising and falling intonation. All this makes it easier for the listener to follow your talk.
8 Did you use rising and falling intonation in your answers to make sure your short talk didn't sound monotonous?		

Learn from mistakes

a   Now watch Video 3. In this recording, one student is giving his short talk about **A new hobby**. Does the student talk about similar ideas to yours?

b   Look at the simplified mark scheme in the **What are the examiners looking for?** section. Answer the following questions and complete the student's mark card.

- What marks would the student get?

- What does the student do well?

- What does the student need to improve?

Student A: Pedro

Grammar: ....

Vocabulary: ....

Development:..

Pronunciation:..

Total mark: ....

Strengths: ....

....

Weaknesses: ....

....

c   Most students find it difficult to develop the ideas in their answers. Look at some sample answers given by students in their short talk about **A new hobby**. The answers are very short. First, think of ways that you could develop them. Then compare your ideas with the suggestions. Now imagine you are the student and give the answers again, but this time make sure they are well developed.

> I think cooking helps you relax, but in volleyball you have to move very fast and you are trying to win so it can be quite stressful.

To develop this answer, you can:

•   explain why cooking is relaxing.

> Many people say cooking is boring, but I do not think so.

To develop this answer, you can:

•   speculate about the reasons why some people think that cooking is boring

•   justify why you disagree and give examples from your own experience when you enjoyed cooking or watching someone else cook.

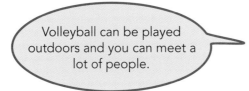

Volleyball can be played outdoors and you can meet a lot of people.

TIP

At the end of your short talk, you should give at least one reason why you prefer one of the options. You can repeat one of the reasons you have already talked about. When you do that, you can introduce the reason with the phrase *As I mentioned earlier … .*

To develop this answer, you can:

- compare and contrast these two aspects (i.e. being outdoors and meeting other people) with cooking.

Cooking is better as a hobby because you can learn useful skills and then turn it into a career.

To develop this answer, you can:

- give examples of the skills you can learn from cooking

- evaluate how useful these skills are in life

- give examples of possible jobs that involve cooking

- evaluate how easy it is to get these jobs in your country

- say whether you think these jobs are a good career choice for young people.

Personally, I would definitely choose playing volleyball as my new hobby because it is better.

To develop this answer, you can:

- explain why it is better.

d Now watch Video 3 again. After Pedro mentions each benefit of cooking, pause the recording and develop his answers with extra ideas of your own. After Pedro gives his answer about playing volleyball, add more ideas of your own to explain why this would, or would not, be a good choice for a hobby.

Remember, to develop all the ideas, you can:

- say what you think about the idea (try to give positive as well as negative points)

- explain why

- give more examples

- speculate why some people might agree or disagree with that

- evaluate how useful the idea is

- compare and contrast this with the other option

- justify your own preference.

Now you are ready to do Test 2, Part 2 (speaking card **Looking after the environment**). Remember to use everything you have learnt so far when you give your short talk.

Test 2

Part 2: Short talk

a   Look at the speaking card **Looking after the environment**. Before you give your short talk, spend one minute preparing what you want to say. Then give your short talk. You should talk for two minutes.

SPEAKING CARD

Looking after the environment

At school, you have been discussing how important it is to look after the environment. You and your family have decided to do something to help the environment. You are considering the following options:

- only buying food that comes from your country

- using less plastic in your everyday life.

How easy or difficult would these options be to do for your family? Say which option you would prefer, and why.

When you have finished giving your short talk about **Looking after the environment**, look at the simplified mark scheme in the **What are the examiners looking for?** section. What marks do you think you would get for your speaking?

Your score for grammar: .... out of 10

Your score for vocabulary: .... out of 10

Your score for development: .... out of 10

Your score for pronunciation: .... out of 10

[Total: 40]

CHECK YOUR PROGRESS

Now think about your progress so far and answer the following questions:

- Was your score in Test 2 higher than in Test 1, or not? Why do you think this is?

- After doing the **Reflection** section, did you find it easier to do Test 2? What guidance did you find helpful?

- Is there anything you still find difficult? What are you going to do to improve this?

Test 1

Part 3: Discussion

a   Look at the **Discussion** speaking card. Give your answers to the questions in the four bullet points. You should talk for 3–4 minutes.

SPEAKING CARD

Discussion

- Is it a good idea for young people to have hobbies?

- Do you think everyone should try to turn their hobby into their job? Why? Why not?

- Some people say that playing sports is the best way to keep fit and healthy. Do you agree?

- There is an opinion that everyone in the family should be involved in preparing meals. What do you think?

TIP

The examiner will ask you up to four questions in the discussion. This means that, if you have a lot to say about some of the ideas, the examiner may only ask you two or three questions.

---

b   When you have finished giving your answers to all the questions on the **Discussion** speaking card, look at the simplified mark scheme in the **What are the examiners looking for?** section. What marks do you think you would get for your speaking?

Your score for grammar: .... out of 10

Your score for vocabulary: .... out of 10

Your score for development: .... out of 10

Your score for pronunciation: .... out of 10

[Total: 40]

Reflection

Now think about the way you did Test 1, Part 3 (**Discussion** speaking card). Read the questions in the following table and put YES or NO to show you have, or have not, done these things. The questions remind you about the things you should do in Part 3 of the Speaking exam. If some of your answers are NO, these are the areas you need to practise a bit more to improve your performance in the exam.

During the discussion (Part 3)	YES or NO	Guidance
1 Did you speak for 3–4 minutes?		
2 Did you give your opinion and explain why you think that?		
3 Did you provide examples to support your opinion?		

4	Did you talk fluently, without pausing for too long?		To avoid long silences while you are thinking of what to say, you can use phrases like *OK, how can I put this?* This will tell the examiner that you are only thinking and are going to continue talking.
5	Did you sound clear?		
6	Did you stress certain words in your answers to emphasise your opinion?		To stress words means that you say them with more force in your voice. You should do this to make sure people pay attention to what you are saying and to make your opinions more powerful.

Learn from mistakes

04

a Now watch Video 4. In this recording, one student is giving his answers to the questions from the **Discussion** speaking card. Are the student's ideas similar to yours?

b Look at the simplified mark scheme in the **What are the examiners looking for?** section. Answer the following questions and complete the student's mark card.

- What marks would the student get?

- What does the student do well?

- What does the student need to improve?

> ## Student A: Pedro
> Grammar: ....
>
> Vocabulary: ....
>
> Development: ....
>
> Pronunciation: ....
>
> Total mark: ....
>
> Strengths: ....
>
> ....
>
> Weaknesses: ....
>
> ....

c Most students find it difficult to develop the ideas in their answers. Also, many students only give their opinion, but forget to give their reasons for it or provide examples from real life. Now look at some sample answers given by students to the four questions from the **Discussion** speaking card. The answers are very short. First, think of ways that you could develop these answers. Then compare your ideas with the suggestions.

Now imagine you are the student and give the answers again, but this time make sure they are well developed.

> I think it is important for young people to do something they like – it provides a good way to relax.

To develop this answer, you can:

- give examples of hobbies and activities

- explain how these hobbies and activities help people relax

- evaluate your own hobbies and how beneficial they are for you.

> Personally, I would love to do a job that is also my hobby, but I do not think it is always possible.

To develop this answer, you can:

- say what is important when deciding what job to do (e.g. the salary, job satisfaction)

- give an example of your hobby

- speculate how likely/unlikely it is that your hobby will become your future career and give reasons for this.

> I only agree up to a point. Sports help you with your stamina, but food is just as important for your health.

To develop this answer, you can:

- speculate about what it means to be fit and what it means to be healthy and whether one is more important than the other

- give examples of activities that help us keep fit and explain why we should do them

- give examples of activities that help us keep healthy and explain why we should do them

- speculate about how easy, or difficult, it is to keep fit and healthy in our modern world.

> It is definitely a good idea. But I know it would not be possible in my family.

To develop this answer, you can:

- give reasons why it would, or would not, be possible to involve everyone in preparing meals in your family

- discuss the benefits of involving everyone in preparing meals and explain what people can learn from it

- discuss how difficult it might be to involve the whole family and explain why.

 d Now watch Video 4 again. After Pedro gives his opinions to individual questions, pause the recording and develop his answers with extra ideas of your own.

04

Remember, to develop opinions, you can:

- give examples

- talk about your own experience

- give explanations for your opinions

- speculate what might happen in the future

- compare and contrast two ideas

- discuss the positive *and/or* negative points of the issue from the question.

Now you are ready to do Test 2, Part 3 (**Discussion** speaking card). Remember to use everything you have learnt so far when you give your opinions in a discussion.

Test 2

Part 3: Discussion

SPEAKING CARD

Discussion

- There is an opinion that the worst pollution comes from plastic. What do you think?

- Do you think companies that harm the environment should be fined a lot of money? Why? Why not?

- Everybody should learn to grow their own food. Do you agree?

- In your opinion, what should supermarkets do with food that is past its sell-by date?

When you have finished discussing your opinions, look at the simplified mark scheme in the **What are the examiners looking for?** section. What marks do you think you would get for your speaking?

Your score for grammar:..................... out of 10

Your score for vocabulary:..................... out of 10

Your score for development:..................... out of 10

Your score for pronunciation:..................... out of 10

[Total: 40]

CHECK YOUR PROGRESS

Now think about your progress so far and answer the following questions:

- Was your score in Test 2 higher than in Test 1, or not? Why do you think this is?

- After doing the **Reflection** section, did you find it easier to do Test 2? What guidance did you find helpful?

- Is there anything you still find difficult? What are you going to do to improve this?

Develop your speaking skills

In the Speaking exam you are tested on the following skills:

1 expressing ideas and opinions on a given topic

2 using a range of words, phrases and grammatical structures

3 producing well-developed answers and maintaining a conversation

4 pronouncing clearly and using intonation to enhance what is being said.

To improve these speaking skills, try the following activities:

- Watch different TV or online debates on a range of topics (e.g. art, sport, the environment) and notice what phrases people use (e.g. to express their opinions, to agree or disagree, to clarify their answers). Then discuss the same topic with a friend. Try to use the same phrases in your discussion.

- Write down a range of linking words/phrases (e.g. *that is why*, *as a result of this*, *however*, *what is more*, *it was not until I got home that*) or a range of vocabulary (e.g. opinion phrases) on cards. Spread out the cards so that you can see what is written on them. Choose a topic and discuss it together with a friend. While you discuss the topic, try to use the linkers or other words and phrases written on the cards. Each time you use a word/phrase on the card, take the card away. Your friend should do the same. After a few minutes, stop and count the words/phrases you have used. The person with the most cards wins. Then discuss the same topic again, but without looking at the cards. Can you still use the same words/phrases?

- Work together with a friend and choose a topic. The first person to start should say a few sentences connected with the topic. The second speaker should continue with the topic and try to add a few more sentences to what has already been said. Continue like this until one speaker has nothing else to say about the topic. The other speaker is the winner.

- Collect a few newspaper headlines about a range of topics. Try to talk about each headline for a few minutes, expressing your opinion about the topic and developing your ideas. When you finish, read the article that came with each headline and compare and contrast the ideas from the article with your own ideas. Tell your friend about it.

- Listen to the recordings from **Listening section 2** to notice how the speakers use intonation in dialogues, short monologues, longer talks and when asking somebody a question and answering a question. Listen carefully to the stress and rising and falling intonation they use. Pause the recording and copy the pronunciation and intonation.

To find out more about how to practise your pronunciation and intonation, you can also use the following book: *English Pronunciation in Use Intermediate* (Cambridge University Press).

Unit 3.3: Language focus

Read the questions on the speaking card. Then go to the **Language focus** sections and follow the instructions on how to answer each question. Do the same for Parts 2 and 3.

Test 3

Part 1: Interview

SPEAKING CARD

Making friends

- What personal qualities make a good friend?

- Can you tell me about your best friend and how you met?

- Do you think that, nowadays, people have a lot of casual friends, but not enough very close friends?

TIP

In the Speaking exam, you are also tested on grammar and vocabulary. To test your knowledge of this, the questions on the speaking card focus on different language features (e.g. narrative tenses when talking about past events).

Language focus

Exercise A: Adjectives and phrases used to describe a friend

a   Look at the first question from the speaking card **Making friends** and give your answer.

What personal qualities make a good friend?

This question focuses on the qualities of a good friend. This means you should use a range of positive adjectives to describe your friend's personality. You could also use longer phrases and relative clauses. To develop your answer, you can also say what qualities you would not like in a friend.

> **Model answer**
>
> I want my friends to be reliable and trustworthy. I also enjoy spending time with somebody who has a good sense of humour and can laugh at things. People who are too serious make me depressed. All of my good friends are very happy people.

b Now watch two students answering Question 1 from the speaking card **Making friends** (Videos 5 and 6). What **adjectives and phrases** do they use? Complete the following table.

	Student A: Lucy	Student B: Nawon
Adjectives and phrases used to describe a good friend		

c Look at some more **adjectives and phrases to describe somebody's personality.** Do they have a positive or negative meaning? Write them in the correct column in the following table. Then look up the meaning of those you do not know in an English dictionary.

generous   moody   somebody who likes to gossip   clever

reliable   easy-going   somebody who has a good sense of humour

bossy   we have a lot in common   they never let me down

greedy   judgemental   somebody who looks down on people

honest   patient   somebody who can keep a secret   stubborn

humble   somebody I can look up to   encouraging   arrogant

Positive meaning	Negative meaning

d Answer the following questions using some of the words and phrases from Exercise **c**. Do not forget to give reasons or include examples of people's behaviour.

1 What are your siblings like? Does their behaviour annoy you sometimes?
2 What makes a good teacher?
3 What makes a bad colleague at work?
4 If you owned a company, what kind of people would you employ?
5 What can you say about your classmates?

CHECK YOUR PROGRESS

Now answer the first question from the speaking card **Making friends** again.

What personal qualities make a good friend?

Remember what you have learnt in this section and try to use it in your answer.

TIP

It is a good idea to record yourself giving your answers before and after you do the **Language focus** sections. It will then be easier for you to see your progress.

Exercise B: Narrative tenses

a Look at the second question from the speaking card **Making friends** and give your answer.

Can you tell me about your best friend and how you met?

This question focuses on something that happened in the past – how you met your best friend. This means you should use a range of **narrative tenses**.

Model answer

When I was walking down the stairs to the school canteen, I dropped some books. One guy came up to me and helped me pick them up. I had never seen him before, but he seemed really nice and we've been friends ever since.

07

08

b Now watch two students answering Question 2 from the speaking card **Making friends** (Videos 7 and 8). What **narrative tenses** do they use? Do the students always use the tenses correctly? Complete the following table.

	Student A: Begum	Student B: Harkomal
Narrative tenses		

c Look at the following table, with the names of the **narrative tenses**. Can you match the tenses with the correct situation when we use them? Then look at the short paragraph that follows and underline all the examples of narrative tenses. Write the examples in the table next to the correct tense.

When I started my new school, I didn't know anybody. One day I was doing my homework in the school library when one of my classmates asked me if I could help him with his homework. I hadn't seen this guy before, so I asked him which class he was in. He told me he was new, just like me. As you can imagine, we had loads to talk about and became really good friends.

Narrative tenses	When to use them	Examples
Past simple	A This tense is used to say something happened or started before another event in the past.	
Past continuous	B This tense is used to talk about events that happened in the past.	
Past perfect	C This tense is used to introduce or describe a scene.	

d Complete the gaps with the correct tense. Use the verbs in the brackets.

1 I .... (try) to concentrate on my homework, but my brother

.... (talk) on the phone so loud that I .... (have to) leave the room.

2 My sister .... (be) so happy when she .... (get) the email

saying that she .... (pass) all her exams.

3 I .... (feel) so exhausted, but happy. I ....

(never / work) so hard in my entire life.

4 Tom and I .... (be) friends for many years, so when he ....

(tell) me he was moving to Australia, I .... (be) really shocked.

5 I .... (walk) to school when I .... (realise) I ....

(leave) my wallet at home.

e Now complete the following sentences with your own ideas. Which tense do you need to use?

1 When I .... , I realised that I ....

2 When I was younger, I ....

3 I had never .... before, but then I ....

4 I was very happy because ....

5 Just as I was leaving home, ...

6 While I .... , my sister ....

CHECK YOUR PROGRESS

Now answer the second question from the speaking card **Making friends** again.

Can you tell me about your best friend and how you met?

Remember what you have learnt in this section and try to use it in your answer.

Exercise C: Opinion, agreement, disagreement, linking words (reason and result)

a Look at the third question from the speaking card **Making friends** and give your answer.

> **Do you think that, nowadays, people have a lot of casual friends, but not enough very close friends?**

This question focuses on people's **opinions**. You should say whether you **agree or disagree** with the idea and **give your reasons why**. You should use a range of phrases to give your opinion, agree or disagree. You should also use a range of linking words/phrases to explain the reasons and results.

> **Model answer**
>
> I couldn't agree more. These days, people have a lot of casual friends thanks to social media. In my view, we are all very busy and don't have enough time to get to know each other, so our only social circle consists of the people we study with or work with. For this reason, we have a lot of acquaintances, but we find it much harder to meet someone new who could also become our best friend.

09

10

b Now watch two students answering Question 3 from the speaking card **Making friends** (Videos 9 and 10). What phrases and linking words do they use? Complete the following table.

	Student A: Jacky	Student B: Harkomal
Opinion		
Agreement		
Disagreement		
Linking words (reason and result)		

c Look at the following phrases. Where necessary, complete the missing words (two of the phrases do not need any completion). Then decide if these are used to **give an opinion, agree or disagree** and write the complete phrase under the correct heading in the following table.

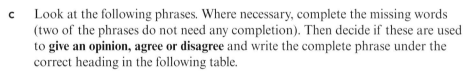

feel   definitely   agree   sure   **think**   right   see

agree   think   seems   point   **support**

1 I .... the same way.

2 The way I .... it, ...

3 For me, ...

4 .... not.

> **TIP**
>
> Remember that the choice of phrases you use depends on the formality of the situation. For example, you should only use the phrases in Exercise **c** that are marked *quite formal* in more formal situations (e.g. in the exam, when giving a presentation at school), not when you are talking to a friend.

5 I feel that …

6 I .... to some extent, but … (*quite formal*)

7 That is (absolutely) ....

8 It .... to me that …

9 I am not so .... about that.

10 I .... so, too.

11 I could not .... more.

12 Personally, I .... that …

13 I cannot .... this opinion, I'm afraid. (*quite formal*)

14 From my .... of view, … (*quite formal*)

Opinion	Agree	Disagree

d Look at the following statements. First, agree or disagree with each statement and explain why. Then give your opinion about the idea.

1 Friends are more important to people than their family.
2 Childhood friendships are stronger than friendships made later in life.
3 True friends never argue.
4 Successful people have more friends.
5 Good friends always share the same hobbies and interests.
6 Close friends should know everything about each other.
7 The more friends you have, the happier you are.
8 Once a friend betrays you, you cannot trust them again.

CHECK YOUR PROGRESS

Now answer the third question from the speaking card **Making friends** again.

> **Do you think that, nowadays, people have a lot of casual friends, but not enough very close friends?**

Remember what you have learnt in this section and try to use it in your answer.

Test 3

Part 2: Short talk

SPEAKING CARD

Work experience

You have been thinking about your future career and what job to choose. To help with the decision, your family has suggested that you should do some work experience. You are considering two options:

- doing a part-time paid job in your local supermarket

- helping your neighbours' young children with their school work.

Discuss the advantages and disadvantages of each option. Say which option you would prefer, and why.

TIP

At the end of your short talk, you should say which option you would prefer. If you like both options equally, you do not have to choose one, but you still have to explain why you like them both.

Language focus

Exercise A: Speculating, adding more information and contrasting ideas

a   After you have read the information on the speaking card **Work experience**, spend one minute thinking about the advantages and disadvantages of the two options:

- doing a part-time paid job in your local supermarket

- helping your neighbours' young children with their school work.

At the end of your short talk, do not forget to decide which option you would prefer and the reason for it.

After one minute, give your short talk.

This question focuses on the **advantages and disadvantages** of two types of jobs. This means you should use modal verbs and other phrases to **speculate about the positive and negative points**. You should also **link your ideas** using appropriate linking words/ phrases to **add more information and to contrast ideas**.

TIP

In some parts of the Speaking exam, you are expected to speculate. This means that you need to imagine some situations that are not really happening in your life. You are asked to talk about what you would do if these things happened to you.

Model answer: advantages and disadvantages

I suppose the good thing about working in a supermarket is that it would give me a chance to meet new people. It might even help me with my communication skills. On the other hand, it's likely to be very tiring, so I might feel too tired afterwards to do my homework. Plus, I don't think it pays much.

And just like the first option, helping somebody with their school work wouldn't pay much either, but I guess the experience would be very useful – explaining something clearly and being organised are important skills. But you'd need to be much better at the subject than the person you're supposed to teach – <u>otherwise, there wouldn't be much point</u> doing this work. <u>Apart from that</u>, people who do this work have to be very patient.

I do think, <u>though</u>, that it's a very interesting idea to try out a few part-time jobs like these to see what you <u>might</u> like to do in the future as your career.

The second part of the question (i.e. at the end of the short talk) focuses on expressing a preference and giving an explanation. This means you should use phrases to say which option you would like better and linking words/phrases to give reasons for this.

Model answer: expressing your preference

Neither of these two options would appeal to me though, but <u>if I had to choose one, I'd probably go for</u> helping somebody with their homework. <u>The reason for this is that</u> I don't like getting up early and this kind of work would most likely be done in the afternoon after school, or in the evening. Also, <u>I'd prefer to do</u> a job where I wouldn't have to talk to many people <u>because</u> I'm rather shy.

When you give your short talk, and any time you talk to somebody, you should also use:

- clear pronunciation
- rising and falling intonation
- emphasis on the words that are important
- short pauses.

This is to make it easy for the person who is listening to you to follow what you are saying. This will also make your speaking more interesting and nice to listen to, just like clear and tidy handwriting makes it easy for people to read handwritten notes and messages.

 b Now look at the first model answer (**advantages and disadvantages**) and listen to the two recordings (Audio tracks 32 and 33). In which recording is the speaker easier to listen to, and why? Listen to the good example again and mark where the speaker rises with their voice and where their voice goes down. Then read the model answer out loud and copy the rising and falling intonation.

c Listen to the good example one more time. This time focus on which words are stressed to add emphasis. Listen carefully and make a dot above words that the speaker stresses. Then read the model answer with the same stress.

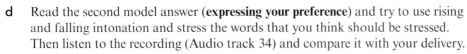 **d** Read the second model answer (**expressing your preference**) and try to use rising and falling intonation and stress the words that you think should be stressed. Then listen to the recording (Audio track 34) and compare it with your delivery.

 e Now watch Student A and then Student B giving a short talk about work experience (Videos 11 and 12). Do you think their intonation and delivery are clear and easy to follow? Why? Why not? Then watch the videos again and focus on the language they use. Complete the following table.

	Student A: Grey	Student B: Ihor
Modal verbs and phrases to speculate about advantages and disadvantages		
Phrases to express a preference		
Linking words/phrases to: • add information • contrast ideas • explain your reasons		

f   Look at the **modal verbs and other phrases** we use **to speculate**. We use them to say how certain we are that something could happen. Can you put the phrases under the correct heading in the following table? Three examples have already been done for you.

> **This would never ...**   It might be the case that ...   It is very likely that ...   This could be ...   I really cannot see how/why ...   It would most definitely ...   It would probably ...   I guess this may ...   It would certainly ...   **It is highly unlikely that ...**   I suppose this would ...

Very certain about something	Not very certain about something	Extremely uncertain about something
It is very likely that ...	*It might be the case that ...*	*This would never ...*

g   Use the phrases from Exercise **f** to speculate about your next school trip. Suggest what destination and activities most students would enjoy, and why.

h   Look at sentences **1–6** and the **linking words/phrases** at the end. Can you match the correct second halves **A–E** to these sentences?

1	I do not fancy going to the cinema – it is really far. Plus, …	A	… I find it fascinating to learn about how people used to live.
2	History is really difficult – there are so many dates to remember. Having said that, …	B	… I listen to music, read and watch films.
3	We all have to do something to protect the environment. That is why …	C	… the tickets are so expensive.
		D	… our family still prefers getting things from the local market – it is more fun.
4	In my free time, I love to spend time with my friends. As well as that, …	E	… I have an important exam coming up, so I do a lot of revising until late at night.
5	The reason why I am so tired these days is that …	F	… I try to avoid using things made of plastic as much as I can.
6	It is so convenient to buy things online. However, …		

i   Read the complete sentences from Exercise **h** and see how the linking words/ phrases are used. Cover up the second halves of the sentences and complete the first halves with your own ideas.

j   Look at some phrases we use to **say what we prefer**. Can you complete the missing words?

1   I would like X .... than Y.

2   X appeals to me .... than Y.

3   I would much .... do X.

4   Personally, I would go .... X.

5   I am not really a big fan .... X, so …

6   I would have .... choose Y because …

k   Use the phrases from Exercise **j** and say which from each of the pairs of two things in the following table you would prefer. Remember to explain your preference.

Going on holiday in the summer	Going on holiday in the winter
Revising for exams on your own	Revising for exams with friends
Spending an afternoon with your family watching a film	Spending an afternoon in the park playing sports with friends
Going to university near where you live	Going to university in another country

I   Discuss the advantages and disadvantages of some more options in the following table and say which one of each you would prefer and why. Remember to use some of the phrases and linking words from Exercises **f, h** and **j**.

Doing unpaid voluntary work for a local charity	Babysitting your younger cousins twice a week
Helping on a local farm to pick fruit and vegetables	Working as a hotel receptionist at weekends
Doing shopping for your elderly neighbours	Helping with some administration tasks at your parents' company

CHECK YOUR PROGRESS

Now give your short talk about **work experience** again. Use the same two options as on the speaking card:

- doing a part-time paid job in your local supermarket
- helping your neighbours' young children with their school work.

Remember what you have learnt in this section and try to use it in your answer.

Test 3
Part 3: Discussion

SPEAKING CARD

Discussion

- Should children regularly get pocket money from their parents? Why? Why not?
- In some cultures, children are expected to do the same job as their parents. Do you think it is a good idea?
- Do you think all people should get paid the same money whatever job they do?
- There is an opinion that some jobs are more suitable for women, while others are more suitable for men. Do you agree?

Language focus

Exercise A: Giving yourself time to think

a   Look at the first question from the **Discussion** speaking card and give your answer.

Should children regularly get pocket money from their parents? Why? Why not?

You will not have any preparation time in this part of the test. However, if you need **to give yourself a bit of time to think** of what to say, there are some useful phrases to do that.

TIP

When you use phrases to give yourself some time to think, do not say them too quickly. Also, try to use these phrases in your everyday conversations to get used to them. Then you will sound more natural when you use them in the exam.

Model answer

Hmm, that's a very interesting question and not something I've thought about before. Personally, I don't get any pocket money. Instead, I have to ask my parents when I need something – not something that I enjoy, to be honest, but I'm planning to get a part-time job soon – just a few hours at the weekend in one of the local shops. So, going back to your question, I guess, by not getting any pocket money, I've been forced to become more responsible and independent. And thinking about it now – if I earn my own money, it'll be much more rewarding. So perhaps, children shouldn't get any pocket money, especially when they become teenagers.

b Now watch two students answering the first question from the **Discussion** speaking card (Videos 13 and 14). How do they start their answer? Do they use any phrases to give themselves time to think? If so, write the phrase they use in the following table.

	Student A: Pedro	Student B: Grey
Phrases to give yourself time to think		

c Look at the following **phrases.** Which of the phrases can you use **to give yourself some time to think?** Put a tick next to these phrases.

1 All in all, I would say that … ☐

2 Well, let me think … I suppose we could say that … ☐

3 What I meant to say was that … ☐

4 To be perfectly honest, this is not a topic I would normally talk about. But I guess … ☐

5 Right, how can I put this …? ☐

6 As I mentioned earlier, … ☐

7 Actually, it has never really crossed my mind … ☐

8 Speaking of which, … ☐

9 I know this has been discussed a lot recently, but, personally, I … ☐

10 Let me put it another way … ☐

d Look at the three questions. Before you give your answers, use some of the phrases to give yourself more time to think.

1 Do you think children should own credit cards?

2 Should students learn about things like budgeting at school?

3 In some countries, people only use their cards or phones, and no cash, to pay for things. Is this a good idea?

CHECK YOUR PROGRESS

Now answer the first question from the **Discussion** speaking card again.

Should children regularly get pocket money from their parents? Why? Why not?

Remember what you have learnt in this section and try to use it in your answer.

Exercise B: Using phrasal verbs and other fixed phrases

a Look at the second question from the **Discussion** speaking card and give your answer.

In some cultures, children are expected to do the same job as their parents. Do you think it is a good idea?

When you give your answers, try to use a wide range of vocabulary, including phrasal verbs and other fixed phrases. In this question, you can use phrases to talk about relationships between children and their parents and getting a job.

Model answer

Well, let me start by talking about my family. My father <u>runs his own business</u> and my mum is a nurse. They've never insisted that I should <u>take up one of their professions</u>. In fact, they've always encouraged me to <u>look into other possibilities</u> and that's the best thing, in my opinion. But I know that some parents do want their kids to follow in their footsteps and it's hard to say 'no' to your parents, but I feel it <u>puts unnecessary pressure on</u> their children.

15

16

b Now watch two students answering the second question from the **Discussion** speaking card (Videos 15 and 16). What phrasal verbs and other fixed phrases do they use? Complete the following table.

	Student A: Polina	Student B: Ihor
Phrasal verbs and other fixed phrases		

c Look at the sentences in the following table. They each have a **phrasal verb** we can use to talk about family relationships, becoming an adult and making an important decision. First, find the correct second half for each sentence and copy it into column B. Then use an English dictionary to find the meaning for each phrasal verb and complete column C.

A	B	C
1 Me and my parents **get** …		
2 My parents have **brought** me …		
3 When I am older, I want to work for an international company and **settle** …		
4 I am so grateful to my parents that they let me **work** …		
5 I definitely want to do the same job as my mum when I **grow** …		
6 Dad actually told me not to go into business. People doing this job often **burn** …		

... **out** because they have so many responsibilities and work such long hours.

... **out** for myself what job I would like to do in the future.

... **up**. Not because she wants me to but because I would really love to be a teacher.

... **on** really well. I can speak to them about anything.

... **up** to be an independent person and think for myself.

... **down** in a big city.

d   Use the phrasal verbs from Exercise **c** to talk about yourself or other people you know. Then say how you feel about these situations and explain why.

CHECK YOUR PROGRESS

Now answer the second question from the **Discussion** speaking card again.

In some cultures, children are expected to do the same job as their parents. Do you think it is a good idea?

Remember what you have learnt in this section and try to use it in your answer.

Exercise C: Giving examples

a   Look at the third question from the **Discussion** speaking card and give your answer.

Do you think all people should get paid the same money whatever job they do?

When you express your opinion, try to support it with a few examples. When you **give examples**, you also ensure that your answers are well developed.

Model answer

I don't think I could support this view because some jobs are more demanding than others. Also, some people need to study for a long time and have a lot of experience before they become good at what they do. Working as a doctor or lawyer <u>are just a couple of examples to illustrate this</u>. They work very long hours and have a lot of responsibilities, and this needs to be reflected in the pay they get. On the other hand, jobs <u>like</u> cleaners or shop assistants are also important, and people work hard in them, but almost anyone can do this type of job. <u>To show you what I mean, let me</u> compare the skills you need in both type of jobs – shop assistants need to be friendly and know what they're selling, but many people can do that. However, lawyers, <u>for example</u>, need to know the law inside out and make quick decisions that can affect other people's lives – and only some people are able to do this. I suppose people's pay should depend on the level of skill they need to do their job.

b Now watch two students answering the third question from the **Discussion** speaking card (Videos 17 and 18). Do they **give** any **examples**? What phrases do they use? Complete the following table.

	Student A: Pedro	Student B: Grey
Phrases to give examples		

c You can use the following phrases to **give examples**, but they each have one mistake in them (e.g. a wrong preposition). Can you correct the mistakes?

1 such like …

2 in example …

3 likes …

4 to show you why I mean …

5 to illustrating this …

6 to give you the idea what I mean …

7 as a proof of …

8 by instance …

d Now discuss different jobs. Remember to support your opinions with **examples** and use some of the phrases from Exercise **c**.

Can you think of jobs where people:

- work very long hours
- have a lot of responsibility
- are underpaid or overpaid
- help others
- work very hard physically
- have to make very quick decisions
- may be replaced with robots in the future?

CHECK YOUR PROGRESS

Now answer the third question from the **Discussion** speaking card again.

Do you think all people should get paid the same money whatever job they do?

Remember what you have learnt in this section and try to use it in your answer.

Exercise D: Clarifying what you have said

a Look at the fourth question from the **Discussion** speaking card and give your answer.

There is an opinion that some jobs are more suitable for women, while others are more suitable for men. Do you agree?

Sometimes, when you express your opinion, the other person may not understand what you are trying to say. When you think your idea/opinion is too long or too complex, you may have to say it again, but using different words to **clarify** it.

Model answer

There's been a lot of talk about equality in the past few years and I'm all up for it. <u>What I mean by this is that</u> it's very important that men and women have the same rights especially when it comes to what jobs they want to do. At the same time, I also believe that some jobs may be more suitable for women than men and vice versa. <u>In other words</u>, we'll probably find more women working as nurses and more men becoming builders or plumbers. However, this doesn't mean that the other gender shouldn't do these jobs. <u>So, I guess what I'm trying to say here is that</u> there are some jobs that may attract one gender more than the other, but that doesn't mean that the other gender shouldn't be allowed to do these jobs if they choose to and if they're good at it.

b Now watch two students answering the fourth question from the **Discussion** speaking card (Videos 19 and 20). While you are watching, decide which idea(s) could be explained a bit more. Then play the video again and pause it where you think you would like to add clarification. Use an appropriate phrase and then clarify the student's idea. Use the following table for your notes.

	Student A: Polina	Student B: Ihor
Ideas from the video that could be clarified		
Phrases you could use to clarify what the student has said		

c Look at some more **phrases** you can use **to clarify what you have said**. They each have one missing word. Can you complete the missing words?

1 .... me clarify that …

2 To put it .... way …

3 What I am suggesting .... is that …

4 Just .... clarify …

5 .... other words …

6 What I mean .... this is that …

d Look at the following statements and express your opinion. Then try to clarify what you have said. Remember to use some of the phrases from Exercise **c**.

- In some jobs women still get paid less than men.

- Women make better teachers.

- Men should be allowed to have time off work to look after their newborn baby.

- Boys and girls should always learn the same skills at school (e.g. cooking and how to repair things).

CHECK YOUR PROGRESS

Now answer the fourth question from the **Discussion** speaking card again.

There is an opinion that some jobs are more suitable for women, while others are more suitable for men. Do you agree?

Remember what you have learnt in this section and try to use it in your answer.

Learn from mistakes

a   Look at the following sentences. They each have mistakes that students at this level often make in their speaking. Can you correct them? The mistakes have been underlined for you.

1   <u>Firstly</u>, we did not love each other, she <u>looks</u> so stubborn.

2   My best friend <u>is living</u> in Italy.

3   She <u>was next on my desk</u>.

4   We can <u>go restaurant</u> together.

5   I also like <u>go to travel</u>, so I want someone who has lots <u>of</u> common with me.

6   It would be quite nice if I <u>have</u> more free time.

7   It <u>might get not</u> that interesting.

8   They do not get <u>pay</u> as much as they should.

9   It is up to the child to <u>follow their parents' steps</u>.

10   <u>Woman were</u> more likely to stay at home with the children, while <u>husband was more working</u>.

b   Now watch the videos from this unit again (Videos 5–20). Use the tick sheet to assess the students' answers to individual questions in all parts of Test 3. Put a tick (✓) if the student does something well and a cross (✗) if the student needs to improve that area.

		Student A	Student B
Grammar	a range of complex structures		
	a range of simple structures		
	minimal errors		
	meaning is clear		

TIP

When you are preparing for the Speaking exam, it is also very useful to watch videos of somebody else doing the exam. When you watch the videos, notice what the students do well and try to copy it in your own speaking. Then focus on their weak areas and try to avoid making the same mistakes in your answers.

		Student A	Student B
Vocabulary	vocabulary is used to express a range of facts/ideas/opinions		
	a wide range of vocabulary		
	precise use of vocabulary		
Development	answers are relevant		
	answers are well developed		
	communication is maintained with no, or very little, support from the examiner		
Pronunciation	clear pronunciation		
	intonation is used		

CHECK YOUR PROGRESS

Now think about your progress so far and answer the following questions:

- When you were doing individual questions from Test 3 for the second time, did you remember to use the language that you learnt in this unit?

- After doing Unit 3.3, do you think that your grammar, vocabulary and pronunciation have improved?

- What marks do you think you would get for your answers in Test 3 now?

Your score for grammar: .... out of 10

Your score for vocabulary: .... out of 10

Your score for development: .... out of 10

Your score for pronunciation: .... out of 10

[Total: 40]

Is there anything that you still find difficult? What are you going to do to improve this?

For more Speaking exam practice, go to Unit 3.4.

Unit 3.4: Test yourself

> **TIP**
>
> Practise for the Speaking exam in pairs with one person being the student and the other being the examiner. The examiner should use the examiner copy of the test, while the student uses the student copy.
>
> First do **Test 4A**. When you have finished, change roles and do **Test 4B**. Record your answers. Then listen and tell each other what you did well and what you can improve.

Test 4A: Examiner copy

Warm-up (1–2 minutes)

Put the student at ease by conducting a short conversation with the following questions:

- How big is your family?

- What films do you like watching?

- What are your plans for the next school holidays?

Part 1: Interview (2–3 minutes)

Tell the student the topic for this part (sports and games). Conduct a short interview with the student by asking the following questions. If the student does not know how to answer the question, ask the question again. If the student still does not know what to say, move on to the next question.

Sports and games

- What sports and games are popular among young people nowadays, and why?

- Can you tell me about a sports day at your school and what you did on that day?

- Do you think that sportspeople make good role models for young people?

Part 2: Short talk (3–4 minutes including 1 minute preparation time)

Ask the student to look at their sheet, which contains the following speaking card. The student has up to 1 minute to read the card and prepare for the talk. The student cannot make any written notes. After one minute, ask the student to start their short talk.

SPEAKING CARD

Endangered animals

Your teacher has asked your class to write a report about an endangered animal. To get more information for your report about the animal, you and your friends are considering the following options:

- organising a class visit to the local zoo

- inviting an animal expert to talk to the class.

Compare the two options and say which option you would prefer, and why.

Part 3: Discussion (3–4 minutes)

Conduct a discussion using the following questions. If the student says very little, encourage a further discussion by asking questions like, *Why do you think so?, Can you tell me a bit more about ...?,* etc. If the student does not know what to say, give them a few seconds, then move on to the next question.

- Some people think that we should not keep animals in zoos. What is your opinion?

- Do you think young people care more about the environment than older people do? Why? Why not?

- There is an opinion that every child should have a pet at home. Do you agree?

- In some countries, students have lessons outdoors, for example, in the forest. Do you think this is a good idea?

Test 4B: Examiner copy

Warm-up (1–2 minutes)

Put the student at ease by conducting a short conversation with the following questions:

- Can you tell me something about your friends?

- Do you prefer watching films or reading books? Why?

- What did you do during your last school holidays?

Part 1: Interview (2–3 minutes)

Tell the student the topic for this part (sports and games). Conduct a short interview with the student by asking the following questions. If the student does not know how to answer the question, ask the question again. If the student still does not know what to say, move on to the next question.

Sports and games

- What sports facilities are there for young people in your local area?

- Can you tell me about a sports competition you took part in and what happened?

- Do you think that doing sports professionally is a good career choice for young people?

Part 2: Short talk (3–4 minutes including 1 minute preparation time)

Ask the student to look at their sheet, which contains the following speaking card. The student has up to 1 minute to read the card and prepare for the talk. The student cannot make any written notes. After one minute, ask the student to start their short talk.

SPEAKING CARD

Endangered animals

In your lessons, you have been learning about endangered animals. You have decided you want to do something about the issue. You are considering the following options:

- giving a talk to other students about the protection of endangered animals

- organising an event to raise money for a charity that helps endangered animals.

Compare the two options and say which option you would prefer, and why.

Part 3: Discussion (3–4 minutes)

Conduct a discussion using the following questions. If the student says very little, encourage a further discussion by asking questions like, *Why do you think so?, Can you tell me a bit more about ...?,* etc. If the student does not know what to say, give them a few seconds, then move on to the next question.

- Do you think charities that help animals are just as important as charities that help people? Why? Why not?

- Some people think that we do not do enough to protect the natural environment. What is your opinion?

- There is an opinion that all zoos should be closed down. Do you agree?

- Many people say that plastic is the biggest threat to the wildlife living in the sea. What do you think?

Tests 4A and 4B: Student copies

Test 4A

SPEAKING CARD

Endangered animals

Your teacher has asked your class to write a report about an endangered animal. To get more information for your report about the animal, you and your friends are considering the following options:

• organising a class visit to the local zoo

• inviting an animal expert to talk to the class.

Compare the two options and say which option you would prefer, and why.

Test 4B

SPEAKING CARD

Endangered animals

In your lessons, you have been learning about endangered animals. You have decided you want to do something about the issue. You are considering the following options:

• giving a talk to other students about the protection of endangered animals

• organising an event to raise money for a charity that helps endangered animals.

Compare the two options and say which option you would prefer, and why.

When you have finished doing the whole test, look at the simplified mark scheme in Section 3, Unit 3.2. What marks do you think you would get for your speaking?

Your score for grammar:...................... out of 10

Your score for vocabulary:...................... out of 10

Your score for development:...................... out of 10

Your score for pronunciation:...................... out of 10

[Total: 40]

> Assessment at a glance and weighting of papers

The information in this section is based on the Cambridge International syllabus. You should always refer to the appropriate syllabus document for the year of examination to confirm the details and for more information. The syllabus document is available on the Cambridge International website at www.cambridgeinternational.org

Reading and writing: Paper 1* (2 hours)

Exercises	Assessment objectives tested	Tasks	Number of marks available (60 marks)
Exercise 1 (Questions 1–6)	R1, R2, R3	Reading comprehension for specific detail	8 marks
Exercise 2 (Question 7)	R1, R2, R3, R4	Multiple matching	9 marks
Exercise 3 (Questions 8–9)	R1, R2, R3	Note-making	7 marks
Exercise 4 (Questions 10–15)	R1, R2, R3, R4	Multiple choice	6 marks
Exercise 5 (Question 16)	W1, W2, W3, W4	Extended writing (informal email)	15 marks
Exercise 6 (Question 17)	W1, W2, W3, W4	Discursive writing (formal/semi-formal article, report, essay or review)	15 marks

* Students are not allowed to use dictionaries.

Listening: Paper 2** (approximately 50 minutes, including the transfer time of 6 minutes)

Exercises	Assessment objectives tested	Tasks	Number of marks available (40 marks)
Exercise 1 (Questions 1–8)	L1, L2, L3	Multiple choice with four visual options (includes monologues and dialogues)	8 marks
Exercise 2 (Questions 9–18)	L1, L2, L3, L4	Multiple choice, short extracts (includes dialogues and monologues)	10 marks
Exercise 3 (Questions 19–26)	L1, L2, L3	Multiple choice, sentence completion (a monologue)	8 marks
Exercise 4 (Questions 27–32)	L1, L2, L3, L4	Multiple matching (short monologues)	6 marks
Exercise 5 (Questions 33–40)	L1, L2, L3, L4	Multiple choice (interview)	8 marks

** Each part of the Listening paper is played twice. At the end of the test, students are given six minutes to transfer their answers onto a separate answer sheet.

Speaking: Paper 3*** (approximately 10–15 minutes)

Parts	Duration	Assessment objectives tested	What happens	Number of marks available (40 marks in total for all three assessed parts)
Introduction	1 minute	N/A	The examiner welcomes the student and explains the procedure.	not assessed
Warm-up	1–2 minutes	N/A	The examiner asks the student a few questions about their life and interests to put them at ease. For example: *What do you enjoy doing in your free time? What are your favourite hobbies, and why? What are your plans for the weekend?* etc.	not assessed

Parts	Duration	Assessment objectives tested	What happens	Number of marks available (40 marks in total for all three assessed parts)
Part 1: Interview	2–3 minutes	S1, S2, S3, S4	The examiner asks the student three questions on the same topic (*e.g. future career*). The examiner may ask questions such as *Can you tell me more about…?* to help the student develop their answers. The student can ask for clarification if necessary.	Assessed
Part 2: Short talk	3–4 minutes (including 1 minute for preparation)	S1, S2, S3, S4	The examiner gives the student a topic card with two ideas (e.g. *learning a new language, learning to cook*) and asks them to talk about the benefits and challenges of each idea. The student is given one minute to think about what they want to say. The student then delivers a short talk comparing and contrasting the two ideas on the topic card. At the end, the student should say which idea they would prefer and explain why.	Assessed
Part 3: Discussion	3–4 minutes	S1, S2, S3, S4	The examiner asks the student questions (e.g. *Do you think learning online is easier than learning in the classroom?*) to further develop the topic used in part 2. The student discusses their ideas with the examiner. The examiner may ask further questions such as *Why do you think this is?* to encourage the student to develop their ideas and opinions.	Assessed

*** The whole of the Speaking test is recorded, including the preparation part. The students are examined individually, **not** in pairs. The examiner and the student must speak in English throughout the whole test. Students are not allowed to write anything down or use dictionaries.

Weighting and assessment objectives

Weighting for qualification		
Assessment objective	0511 and 0991	0510 and 0993
AO1: Reading	25%	35%
AO2: Writing	25%	35%
AO3: Listening	25%	30%
AO4: Speaking	25%	Separately endorsed

Skill	Assessment objectives
AO1: Reading	In the Reading & Writing paper, students will be tested on their ability to: 1 Understand a specific piece of information (e.g. dates, numbers, places) 2 Understand how different ideas are connected (e.g. preference, agreement) 3 Find pieces of information by using the right reading strategy (e.g. scanning) 4 Understand ideas that are implied
AO2: Writing	In the Reading & Writing paper, students will be tested on their ability to: 1 Express facts and opinions clearly 2 Group and link ideas clearly and produce a well-organised text 3 Use a range of words, phrases and grammatical structures 4 Use register (e.g. semi-formal) and style (e.g. a persuasive review, an informative report) appropriate for the given situation
AO3: Listening	In the Listening paper, students will be tested on their ability to: 1 Understand factual information (e.g. names, times, places) 2 Understand more complex ideas (e.g. speakers' feelings and opinions, preferences, decisions) 3 Understand how different ideas are connected (e.g. agreement and disagreement) 4 Understand what speakers imply
AO4: Speaking	In the Speaking paper, students will be tested on their ability to: 1 Express ideas and opinions on a given topic 2 Use a range of words, phrases and grammatical structures 3 Produce well-developed answers and maintain a conversation 4 Pronounce clearly and use intonation to enhance what is being said